AUSTRALIAN LECTURES 1908

AUSTRALIAN LECTURES 1908

BY
ANNIE BESANT

GYAN

ISBN: 978-81-212-1910-5 (HB)
First Published, 1908
Published, 2018
Published by

Gyan Publishing House
5, Ansari Road
Daryaganj, New Delhi-110002
Phone: 011-47034999, 9811692060
www.gyanbooks.com
E-mail: books@gyanbooks.com

Printed at: G. Print Process, Delhi.

Foreword

THE Theosophical Society feels that but brief explanation is needed in offering these lectures to the public of Australasia. This volume has been issued chiefly in response to a wide-spread demand from thousands of people who, having listened to the eloquent voice of one who will live long in their memories as the bearer of a new and encouraging interpretation of life, desire to possess for themselves some permanent record of her message, and who desire that friends in distant parts of this great Continent may also receive some echo of that message.

CONTENTS

PAGE

Theosophy and Christianity 1

Do We Live on Earth Again? 26

Life After Death 55

The Power of Thought ... 80

The Guardians of Humanity ... 110

Nature's Finer Forces ... 136

The Theosophical Society—Branches and Activities

Theosophy and Christianity

In speaking to you on this subject I may, perhaps, preface my remarks with a statement as to the position which is held by Theosophy towards any religion, and not only towards Christianity. Theosophy, which is the Ancient Wisdom on which all the religions of the world without exception are founded, has not, and cannot have, any quarrel with any. Nor, as we consider that every religion, in its own country and among its own people, is the natural way in which that people expresses its method of searching for God, can we in this view ask anyone to leave one religion for another, endeavour in any fashion to proselytise, or carry on what is called missionary work. In coming into the Theosophical Society, a man does not leave his own religion, does not quit his own Church or religious community, is not asked to change his faith, is not asked to renounce his creed. Within the limits of the Theosophical Society we have people of every religion which is known to the world. Members of the Roman Catholic faith make the majority of our Italian and French Sections; members of the Church of England and of Nonconformist bodies the majority of the members of our British Section; members of the Scottish Churches—both the Episcopalian and the Presbyterian—are members of our Society in Scotland; and over in America all the various Nonconformist sects, as well as those of the older Churches, find welcome within the limits of the Society, without challenge and without question. In India, where all the great religions find their representatives, we have Christians and Hebrews, Parsis and Mussulmans, Hindus and Buddhists, Jains and Sikhs, all meeting on the platform of brotherhood, and none seeking to take away his brother's faith, however much he may prefer his own.

That, then, is our position. That which we seek after is Truth, and we do not believe that truth is confined to any one religion, or to any special sect. Over the whole world searchers after truth are found in all the great religions which console man during life and encourage him in the hour of death. And, therefore, in speaking to you, in anything that I may say, I have no desire in any fashion to weaken the hold of Christianity on any who profess that faith. On the contrary, I have known many cases where men and women, puzzled with the problems of existence, unable to solve the difficulties of human life within the limits of the Churches, were leaving the Churches and abandoning Christianity, but came back to it when they found the rational explanations that Theosophy offered of the doctrines which had repelled them. We do not empty the Churches. On the contrary, we bring back to them many of the intelligent and intellectual who have slipped away from them because of the narrow and crude presentment of many a Christian doctrine. We ask people to be more spiritual, to be more liberal, to be more generous towards those with whom they do not agree. We endeavour to spread peace among rival creeds, and to serve every religion in its own country and among its own people.

That, then, is our general position. With regard to any one religion, we try, when we come specially into contact with it, to throw a light on its difficulties, to explain obscure problems, to show its relationship to the other religions of the world, to consider its hold on the intellect and on the heart, and finally to supply to any religion any of its original teachings which in the course of time, by the ignorance of peoples, it has lost, to help that religion to recover the jewels it has lost, and to make its ring of doctrines perfect by recovering the forgotten or the submerged.

Now, just as that is our position towards each religion in turn, so necessarily is it our position towards Christianity. We see at the present time some disadvantages under which it seems to us the faith of Christ is labouring. We see that during the last century, and especially during the last half-century, a very, very large number of the more intellectual and the learned in Western countries have left the Churches. We see, as we turn over Church papers and Nonconformist papers, that they are always complaining of the lessening influence of their particular form of Christianity. Above all, they complain that while very many women come to their places of worship, men are apt to be conspicuous by their absence. We notice, also, that they complain that the manual labour classes are very little found in touch with the churches and chapels, and so on. And we cannot help thinking, anywhere where that is the case, that there is something lacking, not in the religion itself, but in the presentment of that religion to the minds and hearts of those who ought to be its people. Looking at it in this way, we ask ourselves: "May it not be possible that Theosophy may bring to Christianity some new reinforcement, some help, which will restore its sway over the mind of the philosopher as well as over the mind of the more uncultivated and less thoughtful man? Is it not possible that in the way Christianity is put, having in view the growing intelligence, the growing conscience of the time, there may be some things that shock the conscience and some things that outrage the intelligence? May it not be that it has been a great mistake, that chiefly among the so-called Protestant communities since the time of the Reformation, religion, the Christian religion, has been brought down too much to one level, and that a low one?" You continually find it stated, even by the clergy, ministers of the Churches, that their object is that all they say shall be intelligible to the least cultivated amongst their hearers, that religion ought to be easy, that it ought to be intelligible to the man of smallest knowledge, of least education. And it is said to be the pride of the modern Christian, not of the older, that the most ignorant man can understand all that Christianity has to teach. Now, that is not true. If it were true, it would be the knell of Christianity. For no religion can afford to leave the thoughtful and the cultured, the philosopher and the metaphysician, with nothing to be said to them. The form of belief that suits the peasant, the ignorant and uncultured man, is a form that must inevitably repel the thoughtful, the artistic, the cultured, and the intellectual. Why should the noblest subject on earth be brought down to the level which is that of the child and the ignorant? I am not going to say that the child and the ignorant should be neglected. I admit that every religion worthy the name has as much to give to the child and the ignorant as those narrow minds are able to receive. But I refuse to say that the Water of Life must only be poured into the thimble, and not into the larger vessel of the trained intelligence and the opened spiritual nature. You have no right to alienate knowledge while you cater for those who are ignorant. By all means give them that which will brighten their lives; by all means give them that which will illuminate, alleviate, and console; but do not deny to the very flower of your generation that you have anything to give them which they alone are capable of receiving. For it was not so in the elder days. In the early days Christianity had not only its little children, not only the sick who were in need of medicine, but also its great philosophers, its mighty doctors of the Science of the Spirit, its deep conceptions for the highly cultivated, its profound mysteries for the spiritual man. That cannot be a matter of question to anyone who knows the literature of the early Church. Nor can it be a matter of question even to the careful reader of the New Testament. It was St. Paul himself, one of the greatest teachers that the Church has produced, who stated: "I speak wisdom among those that are perfect;" St. Paul who declared that he had fed them with milk as babes in their early stage, but that they ought to be ready now for something more than children's food; St. Paul who, when he was speaking to one of the early Bishops, St. Timothy, reminded him of the wisdom in which he had been instructed, and told him to impart it also to men who were wisely chosen. For babes in the Word, certainly the milk that nourishes;

but for the perfect, the wisdom which illuminates. And why should modern Christianity deny to those who can understand it the great mysteries of Christianity, and only give the milk for the babes, and refuse to the grown-up Christian the nutriment necessary for the growth in him of the spiritual life? Why has it ceased to "speak wisdom among them that are perfect"?

And that phrase, "The perfect," is a phrase upon which I want for a moment to dilate. It is a very well-known phrase, at least among very large numbers of men—the perfect, the perfecting, the making perfect—and it is now, and always has been, connected with what is called "initiation," to which the profane, as they are sometimes called, are not admitted, but only those who are ready for the mysteries which are given. Now I know, of course, that in these allusions I am alluding to knowledge which has largely vanished, to empty vessels which are not now filled with the deep knowledge of ancient truths. But the very existence of what is called Freemasonry amongst you, with its initiatory ceremonies, with its exclusion of the unilluminated, with its gradually building up to the high stage of the Master, with its perfecting in yet higher degrees, is all a shadow that has come down to modern days of things that were realities in the early days of Christianity, those mysteries which are the very root of every esoteric religion, and the loss of which takes away from the religion much of the value which it ought to have for its higher disciples. And coming to that phrase, "the perfect," which St. Paul used, how many other allusions there are in his epistles to these gradations of Christian knowledge. Over and over again he speaks of these hidden things; over and over again he makes allusions which only the initiated can understand in their full value.

Pass, however, from St. Paul and his many dark sayings, as is said by one of his fellow-Apostles, and look at the Church in the days of its great power, when it was taught by those who had first-hand knowledge, and not only by those who spoke by a book or tradition. Do you know that in the early Church no man was allowed to hold the office of Bishop, unless he had been initiated into the Mysteries of Jesus, that no man was allowed to take that high office of the Shepherd of the flock unless he had first-hand knowledge of the truths it was his duty to proclaim? Read the statements of those early Bishops of the Church. See how one of them declared that they were "taught by angels." See how some of the opening words of initiation into the Mysteries were given, how the conditions of that admission were laid down, how it was proclaimed by the Hierarch who opened the door of those Mysteries that only those might come forward to be admitted who "for a long time had been conscious of no transgression," and who were competent for the teaching of the Word. See how he offered knowledge to those who were fit to receive it, and summoned such to enter the Mysteries, wherein, it is said, "is given the teaching in secret by Jesus to His disciples."

Now, what has become of that great teaching Christ gave to His own disciples, His own apostles—the teaching which was not given to the outside public who came to listen to Him? He said: "To them I speak in parables, to you it is given to know the mysteries of the kingdom of God." And we find in the records of the early Church that these secret teachings were handed down, not committed to writing, but handed down from teacher to pupil, from mouth to ear, as it was said—always by word of mouth. They were handed down century after century, so that as late as the time of Origen we find him alluding to them, and declaring that the Church possessed in its treasures the secret teachings which Jesus had given "within the house" to His apostles, and not outside to the mass of the listening people. Where are they now? What has become of them, of those inner teachings which were given in the Mysteries and have made a knowledge of God possible to the human soul? On this you may turn over page after page of information in those early writings of the great teachers of the Church. Remember how Origen declared that while the Church had medicine for the sinner, it was not on sinners that the Church of Christ could be built up. He declared that what the Church needed in order that it might be strong were what he called the Gnostics. But where are the Christian Gnostics now?

That word has a very definite meaning. The deepest was the knowledge of the superphysical and the Supreme—not the teaching about them, not the talking about them, not the believing in them, but the direct individual knowledge. The Gnostic was the man who knew, not the man who believed. The mass of the Christian congregation were believers; the teachers and leaders were the Gnostics, the knowers. And they only dropped out of the Christian Church with the decay of learning which accompanied the decay of the Roman Empire and the Eastern Byzantine Empire that took up the work, after the decay of that knowledge, after the incursions of barbarians swept over Europe and gave ignorance in the place of knowledge. Then, and then only, was it that an ignorant majority declared the Gnostics to be heretics, the knowers to be outside the pale of orthodox Christianity. Since that time Christianity has lost its power, though not all its knowledge. No longer do you find among them those who have the "signs of an apostle." No longer do you find among them the power to heal, the power to open the eyes of the blind, to make the lame walk. All these powers are gone with the knowledge which was cast out of the Church in the days of its ignorance, and only here and there in the darkness shines out the light of some Saint, who by knowledge had rewon the powers, the solitary infrequent shining of the Spirit which had found its way to the light, where the official guardians had closed the doors against it. And so you find gradually the knowledge came into fewer and fewer hands, and a priesthood grew up who were not the leaders of men to knowledge and the teachers of the Way, but who rather claimed to have the right to bar the way themselves, and claimed authority rather because they believed than because they knew. And so more and more heresy arose, and when science came back to Europe, the Church opposed it. And so the great gulf began to be widened between knowledge and religion, between science and Christianity—a gulf that has grown wider and wider as the years have rolled on, until there is danger, though a danger that I hope has passed, that the intellect of Christianity shall be divorced from its faith, and that only those who do not care to understand shall crowd the seats of Christian Churches. A change is coming over Christendom, a marked and wonderful change. Contrast the Christendom of to-day with the Christendom of 50 years ago. See how liberal thought has grown. See how new interpretations of doctrines are becoming current. See how the crude, literal interpretation has disappeared, or is to be found amongst the more uneducated people only, and how loftier thought and nobler spirituality, a deeper understanding of the great teachings of Christianity, is spreading through the Churches and making everywhere its voice to be heard.

Let us see whether in this movement that we call Theosophy there is not something of value for Christians in its dealing with Christian doctrines, and whether, in fact, that growing liberality is not very largely the outcome of the spreading of Theosophy within the Church itself. For up and down through the country now we hear Theosophy preached from the pulpits. Up and down through Christendom we find clergy and priests who are drinking at the fountain of the ancient knowledge, and are beginning again to give it to their people. Mystic Christianity is coming back. Spiritual interpretations are everywhere being offered, and the crude literalism that killeth is dying, while the spirit that giveth life is making itself felt throughout the Churches. To see how Theosophy deals with this, let us take one or two doctrines and look at them from the theosophical standpoint, and see how a Christian may grasp that further teaching and find his own truth become more beautiful and more inspiring than it was in his narrower days.

Let us take, for instance, the great doctrine of the Atonement. That has gone through very many stages in the Christian Church, as every student of Christianity knows full well. In the very early days of Christianity it took on a very peculiar form, or peculiar from the standpoint of the modern student. It was not possible in the days which were near the days of the Christ—that Revealer of God, so full of tenderest compassion, of all-embracing love—while His personal influence was over the minds of His followers, to regard the Father, whose love He revealed, as a wrathful Judge and condemner of the whole human race. It was not possible to those more spiritual Christians to regard the sacrifice of the Divine Son as a sacrifice offered to propitiate the wrath of an angry Father. There is no trace of that through all the literature of the early Church. On the contrary, the sacrifice of death that was offered was held to be a sacrifice for the ransoming of man from the power of Satan, and the argument that you may read at leisure, if you desire, is that God, being just, could not fail to give even Satan his due, and that as man had fallen under the power of Satan and become a bond-slave of the Devil, it was necessary to ransom him justly from the Lord of Death into whose hands he had fallen, and so Christ sacrificed Himself and gave His life, a ransom for many, after death going down into the domain of the ancient foe to rescue from him the myriads of men who had passed away before the coming of the Christ, and redeeming them from the hell that had engulfed them, He led them up into Paradise as a reward won by His own sacrifice, paid in His own death. That was said to be the Atonement, and why His death was necessary. It was a ransoming of men from Satan, to redeem those under death's power. But gradually that view, which is still on record, as you may read for yourself, passed out of the mind of Christendom, largely, I think, because men grew more cruel in their ignorance, and gradually, instead of a loving Father revealed by the Christ, there grew up the terrible figure of an angry God. And so you come to that mark in the history of the Atonement, the famous work of Anselm the Archbishop, "The Wrath of God to Man." That is the title of the book —in Latin, of course—that the teaching, then, of the Church. And so Christ became a sacrifice to God, who sent Him to redeem the world. As that idea grew and flourished, and it became the doctrine of the Atonement in the Christian Church, spreading everywhere and influencing all men's minds, it became deeply rooted as an essential teaching of Christianity. If you take the time of the so-called Reformation, there is nothing to choose between Roman Catholicism and Protestantism in the way they put this particular doctrine. Luther, Melanchthon, and Calvin put it as harshly as had Anselm the Archbishop. If you trace it down these different lines you will find it keeps the same idea of a substitutionary sacrifice, which had become legal, not spiritual—a legal substitution, not a spiritual identity of nature. And coming down even to the days when those of my own age were young, you will find Bishops of the Church of England, teachers of all the religious communities, preaching this same doctrine of substitutionary Atonement, and of the wrath of God pacified by the sacrifice of Christ.

But within the bosom of the Christian Church itself rose revolt against that doctrine. The note was struck by the Broad Church Party, as it was called in the days of my youth. You have a very beautiful book coming out of the bosom of the Presbyterian Church in Scotland,

"The Nature of the Atonement," by Macleod Campbell, in which he describes the Atonement as meaning the self-revelation of God to man in the person of the man Jesus, and the showing to God what men might be in the perfect manhood of the great Teacher—a step in advance, getting rid of the idea of sacrifice being needed to propitiate the changeless love which rules the worlds. From that time onward the doctrine has changed in its aspect. Different sects of Christians put it forward in different ways, and only rarely now do you find the old legal substitution, the old idea that the wrath of God needs the sacrifice of his own Son to quench it. Still, it is incorporated in the Articles of the Church of England, and in other confessions of Christian Churches.

What view would Theosophy put forward as the true view of the Atonement? Theosophy would say that Christ symbolises a certain stage of the unfolding of the Divine Spirit in man, a stage at which unity is practically realised—when the Spirit in all forms is known as one. It would say that He whom you call the Christ, having reached that stage of utter unity with God and man alike, it became possible for Him to share with man His purity and to share with man man's weaknesses, by virtue of a perfect identity of nature. By a perfect humanity and a realised divinity, that union that He knew and realised, He was able to be one with His brethren in human form. As the sun shining in the heaven far above all the obstructions of earth can pour down his life and heat into many a garden and many a yard shut in from other gardens and other yards by the walls that obstruct on the surface of the earth, but all open to the light of heaven, as the sun can pour his light unhindered into all these receptacles separate from each other down here, so can the Son, so can Christ, pour down His life, His purity, His perfect humanity, into all the separate forms of human beings, separate to each other, but open to Him in the glory of His unity, the perfection of His life. We are separate the one from the other; yes. Barriers are between us, and separateness to us is more real than unity. But Christ has grown above all the barriers and looks down alike into all the forms, can pour His spirit into them, His purity, His love—can help them to be what He is, by virtue of that unobstructed communication. He not only shares His purity with them, but also shares their sin. That is the greatness of the truly spiritual nature. The spiritual man who has reached the stage of a Christ cannot separate himself from the lowest, vilest criminal. There is one spirit in the criminal and in the Son. He cannot reach full perfection while one human being remains sinful. And so it is truly laid down in the Christian Scripture: "He made Him to be Sin for us." In the light of that mighty unity there is no ascribing of the sin of one to the righteousness of another, but a perfect sharing alike for all. That is the glory of the Christ. He sees no difference; He knows no separateness. He has become one with all humanity. His righteousness theirs, and their imperfections His. Truly is it a wonderful Atonement, a making one of higher and lower; and it makes oneness by lifting the manhood into divinity, making pure all who realise the oneness. But to us the Atonement is not necessarily possible only to one Christ. He is the first-born among many brethren. This is a point where many of the Christians would differ from us. There is many a Christian man to-day who would accept that view of the Atonement, and realise that it means identity of nature and not substitution. But there are only some who are willing to admit that that high rank of spiritual greatness can be reached by more than one who is at once man and God. The greatness of the conception that all men are divine staggers them, and feeling their own weakness, their own imperfection, their own sinfulness, it comes as a shock for us to say to them: " But you also one day will be a Christ." But if it were not so, of what value would be the coming of these mighty ones, in whom God is made manifest in the flesh? For if They were different in Their nature, what help would Their example be to us? Were They not identical with us in manhood and divinity, how could They elevate Their brother man to God? The guarantee that you have it within you, the promise of your own future Christhood, lies in that command breathed to His disciples by Christ Himself: " Be ye therefore perfect, even as your Father in Heaven is perfect." Those words cannot fail. If Christ be indeed all that we believe Him to be, His lips could not speak a falsehood. His command could not remain an empty form of words. Nothing less than Divine perfection is the future of each one of you. How quickly will you win it? Ah, that is within your own power. How swift or how slow your climbing, that is for your own will to decide, for the Divine Will never forces the human will, which is part of itself, and that separate will must realise its unity before perfection can be consciously realised. But none the less, it lies in the future for every child of man; none the less, that perfect will shall not remain unaccomplished, and despite our feebleness and our folly, despite our pettishness and our childishness, we are none the less sons of the immortal Love, to grow up to that perfection of Christhood, and thence to rise to the perfection of God Himself. In that way does Theosophy look at this great doctrine of the Atonement. That there is some mighty truth in it, even the man who most rebels against its cruder form ought to be willing to acknowledge, for it has wrought so much of inspiration, has brought out so much love in the human heart, has proved so inspiring to so many noble souls, that you may be sure there is a spiritual kernel within the husk of the crude and literal interpretation.

Pass from that and take another doctrine, that of Prayer. Now, what is prayer? Many definitions of it have been given, and it ranges from the smallest physical petition put up by a starving man to the highest contemplation of the loftiest saint entranced with the beauty of divinity. The whole of that conception is covered over by the one word, "Prayer," and so confusion has arisen with regard to it, and many attacks crudely made. None the less is prayer a mighty force, a thing to be understood and utilised. Prayers which are simply petitions for physical things are the lowest grade of prayer, but none the less may such prayers be answered without any interference with law. Some of you may remember how, 20 or 30 years ago, scientific men who were then leading European thought declared that prayer must be futile because it was an attempt to change the laws of nature. But how is it an attempt to change the laws of nature—even a petition, say, for daily bread? The reason why that was thought was because popular Protestantism had omitted the whole world of life except the human life at one end and the Divine life at the other, and a great gulf between. They had done away with all those innumerable intelligences who occupy the ladder of existence from the lowest to the God. They saw nothing save lives on the physical world and the supreme Life, and so naturally, seeing nothing between them, they thought that every prayer, if it reached at all, must reach the Supreme Will, and thus was trying to change that changeless Will and alter the laws of Nature which are an expression of Himself. But that is not so. There is nothing more of breaking the law in prayer than there is in the child who asks something of its father and mother. You do not feel that the law of nature has been broken, if the child asks you to give it something which it cannot reach for itself. You do not go into long scientific arguments, as many of my Free Thought friends have done—and as I did in the early days—in order to show that if rain were given in answer to a prayer, you would have to change the whole course of events from the beginning of the globe down to the present day. Sir Oliver Lodge has answered that very well. He said: "You do not alter a law of nature when you ask the gardener to water your garden." Why is it breaking a law of nature when you ask the higher intelligence to pour down rain on a thirsty soil? It is not the breaking of a law, but the utilising of a law which is not under the control of the human intelligence, but is under the control of higher intelligences, call them what name you like—angels, or anything else. The point to realise is that there are beings above us who are not yet God Himself, endless grades of superhuman intelligences, who administer the laws of nature, who influence the lives of men. They have slipped too much out of the sight of the ordinary Protestant. The ordinary Roman Catholic has never, of course, let go his hold on the doctrine of angels. No religion that I know of in the world is without this doctrine as a practical daily fact except certain Protestant communities who have lost sight of it merely by reaction. For no other reason, for it is the most rational doctrine in the world, that there are beings around you who may be appealed to and may give help, that when the prayer goes up to God those who are His ministers and His servants are the immediate agents by whom that prayer is answered, and that it is true and not false that prayer has a great power even in the physical affairs of man. It is a utilising of the laws of consciousness, of the powers of thought, which are now being investigated so largely. Those who know how to utilise thought, know that it is not at all necessary to put it into the form of prayer in order to bring about that which they desire to achieve. A prayer for physical needs is only useful as "prayer," because it helps to concentrate the mind, to bring out the strenuous action of the human soul behind the prayer, to appeal to some outside intelligences for help, as the father or mother is appealed to by the child. All these things are within the laws of nature. They are all uses of the laws of nature. Those who know more of law than we do, who are stronger than we are, can utilise laws of nature which are for the most part beyond our grasp for the present; but as we also learn the power of thought and the control of nature, we bring about by our own motion exactly the same results as are brought to you by prayers for physical things.

To pass away from the lowest type of prayer, let us see what prayer is in its higher forms. It is the necessity of the spiritual life. It is the opening up of the whole nature to higher things. There are always playing upon you the love and wisdom of the Supreme God, bathing you in their atmosphere as you are bathed in the air around you. But you can shut your windows against the air, you can shut your doors against the sunlight, and neither sunlight nor air can enter through the closed window and the closed door. They are always there, and all you have to do is to open the window and to open the door, and then the light and the air will stream in and give you light and help. So with prayer. It is the opening of the windows of the spirit; and it is the throwing wide open the doors of the spiritual nature; it is putting yourself into a receptive attitude, and holding up empty hands to the everlasting fulness, which can fill them with its blessings and its life. That is the value of prayer, and everyone who strives to lead the spiritual life, as they develop the spiritual power, knows the priceless value of the prayer that opens up avenues between man and God, or, to speak more accurately, the avenues between the God within you and the God without. That is prayer in the higher sense. One reason why it makes a man nobler is because you inevitably become that which you think. As you contemplate Divine purity, Divine wisdom, Divine love, those qualities reproduce themselves in your nature, and awaken divinity within you, sleeping in the innermost of your being. So do not let any crude scientific arguments shake your hold on the great reality of prayer. Realise that it means keeping open the avenues between earth and heaven, between the lower and the higher life, that although prayers may often be childish, even then they are not cast out by the Supreme Heart. For what mother leaves her child forlorn because the infant lips cannot articulate clearly, but can only babble with baby tongue the wants that it craves to have supplied. As the mother heart to the child, so is the Divine Heart to all His children, and even the broken accents of the infant bring back response from that Universal Love. So, prayer is not one of the things to be cast aside in your growth. It is a thing to raise, to purify, to make nobler and more spiritual, to make the transforming change of man into God, to make you after the likeness that in meditation you adore.

But has Theosophy nothing to say to Christianity except explanations and defences against attack of its own great doctrines? It seems to us that Theosophy has some other work that it can do for the many Christian Churches, and that is to give back to them something of what they have lost—not only what I spoke of in the beginning, the bringing about a restoration of the great Mysteries which are necessary for the triumph of Christianity—but also to bring back the way to the gaining of knowledge, and one or two doctrines that have slipped out of sight.

I do not want this evening to argue with you as to the great doctrine of reincarnation, as I have done that elsewhere, but what I would urge upon you is that this part of the Christian heritage is not a doctrine that you should take from Hindu or Buddhist, not a doctrine that you should borrow from Greek, Roman, or Egyptian, but a doctrine that belongs to you in your own religion.

It is part of the early teaching of the Christian Church. It has been taught in many forms, this pre-existence and re-birth of the soul. It has been given in many different ways to the world, and there were many ways in the early Christian Church in which the doctrine was spoken of and taught. Tertullian puts it in a curious way. He speaks of many deaths and many resurrections, and makes that phrase in the Christian Creed, "The resurrection of the body" to apply to reincarnation, that each man rises over and over again in a new body. He argues in a well-known passage that after a while we shall escape from the repeated deaths and repeated resurrections, and attain to the final resurrection—the immortal life. So that famous verse in the Book of the Revelations some thinkers apply to the doctrine of reincarnation, when it is declared of him that overcometh, "I will make him a pillar in the temple of my God, and he shall come out no more." You find that regarded as meaning not going out again into life by reincarnation, but a remaining for ever consciously in the Divine Presence. So, again, you find Origen arguing that you could not justify the justice of God with regard to Jacob and Esau, unless you admitted that they had lived before, and that in those previous lives they had shown the qualities which drew in one case the Divine blessing, and in the other case the Divine displeasure. And so on, through one writer after another, showing you how this doctrine is part of the faith once delivered to the Saints. True, it fell out of the greater part of the Church; and with that came all the teachings against which the modern conscience has revolted. It is not only important as a doctrine by itself. It is important also in the many results that inevitably follow its acceptance or rejection. If, for instance, reincarnation be the view of the Christian Church, what effect has that on hell and on heaven? They become exactly what they used to be—temporary conditions; and so they become rational instead of irrational.

As to the doctrine of hell, which in modern Christianity has become a doctrine of everlasting torture, against which the conscience of Christianity revolts, that monstrous doctrine that in this little life of ours—so brief, so small—we can deserve an everlasting condition of torture, unutterable, irremediable—not only needless, but purposeless, with nothing to come out of it, no results, no fruit—very few Christian people believe in that to-day. They cannot believe in it, for they feel that no man is vile enough to be punished with everlasting hell. If you are frank and honest with yourselves, you know also that none of you deserve an everlasting condition of bliss. You are not big enough for it. Your crimes are not big enough for hell, nor your virtues for heaven. You have to learn. You have to grow. You have to become very much bigger than you are, much more grown up—not the children that we see around us everywhere, with your greatest pleasures in sport of every sort, with the petty ambitions of ordinary men. These are all toys for children, not for everlasting spirits. What has heaven to give you? How can you say you are ready for it? Out of the horror of an everlasting hell the revolt has grown, and that horror is only a result of losing hold of the great doctrine of reincarnation. For, mind, there is a truth in hell. The man who keeps on doing evil must suffer for the evil he does.

That is the law. You cannot get away from the results of your own actions. You cannot, if you are a drunkard all your life, change by a moment's repentance into a spirit fit for the Kingdom of Heaven. If you have committed a murder you cannot make peace with God with the shadow of the gallows over you, and go to the gallows saying you are sure of God's forgiveness. There is no way out of that, if you believe in hell. You must make all these excuses to get people out of it. However wicked a man is, we are bound to make some escape for him, rather than say he has gone into the misery that never will end. If you believe in reincarnation you say that the suffering that follows evil, and is its inevitable result, is remediable, educative, and purifying, so that the man is the better, nobler, and purer for it. Heaven becomes rational when it is temporary, and when in that heaven you can become better than when you left the earth. If it be a time when you can change into faculty all the experiences you gathered here, then heaven becomes a rational condition of existence. Reincarnation makes it possible, inevitable. When you come to think of it, these two absurd doctrines of an everlasting heaven and an everlasting hell are both utterly opposed to the belief in reincarnation. "You have only got one life. You must make the most of it. You must try to cram everything into it ;" whereas, if you have many lives and plenty of time, you can build up that perfection to which you aspire. Hence by bringing back to Christendom the doctrine of reincarnation, we destroy the everlasting hell and the everlasting heaven, and give back to human life that strength and that dignity which come out of the knowledge of an eternal state. What we call the law of Karma, the law of cause and effect, is put very well by St. Paul in the Epistle to the Galatians: " Be not deceived, God is not mocked. Whatsoever a man soweth, that shall he also reap." That is what we call the doctrine of Karma, that every man reaps exactly as he sows. If he wants to reap happiness, he must sow happiness; if he wants to reap purity, he must sow pure thoughts, pure words. pure deeds; if he wants to reap nobility, he must sow noble thoughts. Then he will come to have them. How can you reconcile that doctrine of every man reaping as he sows with the doctrine of a substitutionary atonement? In this we can appeal to the Christian's own Scriptures, and throw them back upon the teachings of their own great apostle. In recalling this doctrine of Christianity, we are giving them, as I said, their own back again. For just as sometimes family jewels get put away, covered with dust, and forgotten in some old coffer, or some hidden chamber, so many of the jewels of their own Christian faith, their own heritage, their own property, have become lost and laid away, and all the Theosophists need do is to bring them out of the place where they have lain forgotten, wipe off the dust of ages, and give you back your own. That is the Theosophist's duty. That is what he has learnt—that his mission to the Christian world.

And so I come back in the end to the point I put to you at the beginning, that we do not ask you to leave your faith, that we do not desire to win you from your allegiance to the Christ, that we do not desire to take away from you one doctrine that has helped, alleviated, and consoled. We only desire to deepen your knowledge, to widen your thought, to make more real your spirituality, so that you may give to the world what Christianity has to give, that you may drop the bigotry and fanaticism, the narrow-mindedness, which are obstacles in the spreading of the spirit of the Christ, and that you may realise that those who, under many names, and in many religions, worship the spirit of truth and love, are your brothers, not your enemies, and although you may call them heathen, they are in truth the children of God, and share in the worship of the Christ.

Do We Live on Earth Again ?

A few days ago I received a request that in the lecture I was about to give I would try to explain the puzzle of life. The writer remarks: "Life is largely chaotic, puzzling, topsy-turvy, almost hopeless. What grounds are there for thinking that the next, or any other succession of lives, will be any better, more orderly, purposeful, just, or right? If the vital principle persist, may it not be amid conditions and surroundings quite as blundering, unequal, unfair, and abortive, as the present existence is?" When I read that postcard I thought that when I was speaking on the subject of Reincarnation, I might very well try, in fact must inevitably try, to answer the question which is there propounded, for the injustices, the inequalities, the apparently purposeless sufferings of life are the things that drive many thoughtful and intelligent people into scepticism and despair. If I can succeed in showing you to-night that, according to the most ancient and the most philosophical view, life is not such a hopeless chaos as too many believe it to be to-day, if I can show you that there is an underlying principle, that for every man and woman there is hope and not despair, then, to some extent at least, I shall have answered the question propounded, and shall, perchance, set some of you on the road which makes life intelligible, which shows the plan of evolution and enables all to understand something of their own destiny, and something of the possibilities of human life.

Now there is a tendency among people, inevitably, to regard the views of their own time, and of those who immediately surround them, the views of the religion into which they were born, as being the only reasonable view of life. We are all content to be more or less what is called "parochial," to think that the public opinion of our time is the only public opinion worth considering, to think that the views natural to us and to our nation are the only views that reasonable men should consider; and it is because I am aware of the dead weight of this pressure of prejudice that I would open what I have to say to you to-night by reminding you that the modern view of human life, in its narrowness and its limitation, is a view that has only been accepted for some hundreds of years out of the many, many thousands during which humanity has thought and laboured. There is no philosophical doctrine which has behind it what I have sometimes called so magnificent an intellectual ancestry as the doctrine of reincarnation; none for which there is such weight of the opinion of the wisest of men; none, as Max Muller declared, on which the greatest philosophers of humanity have been so thoroughly in accord. I do not put it to you that you ought to accept any teaching because of the weight of authority of the great minds that have regarded it as true, because I thoroughly admit that until a doctrine approves itself to your own intelligence and conscience it is not true for you, however true it may be from another's standpoint. It is not then that I want to impose upon you the weight of authority, but only to win your careful listening and thoughtful attention to the truths which have been endorsed by the greatest minds of humanity; only for the sake of reminding you, as against the brief period of prejudice and narrowness of the time, how long the belief of reincarnation has existed, and how great are the minds of those who have accepted it. For there is no religion, among all the great religions of the world, which has not built upon this doctrine its theory of morality and its theory of immortality. It does not matter to which of the great religions you go, you find overwhelming evidence on this line. I need hardly mention that most ancient religion of Egypt, for you all know that, in the Egyptian creed, the whole life of man on earth, in other worlds, in the heavenly region, coming back again to this world, was traced in the minutest details, step by step. I need hardly remind you that in Chaldea and Assyria the same doctrine was taught some 9000 or 10,000 years before the Christian era. I might take you to China, and point out to you how there the same idea prevailed; or I might leave the dead religions and bring you to the living, and remind you how in India the Hindu faith, one of the most widely spread in the world, is, from beginning to end, moulded and shaped in its conception of human life by this idea of reincarnation. The same that is true of Hinduism is true of Buddhism. And when you have named those two religions you have more than half the inhabitants of the world to-day accepting this great philosophy. If you turn to a religion more familiar to you, that of the Hebrews, and ask the great historian Josephus what was the belief of the Hebrews, you will find how he lays it down that every soul that had not reached perfection had to return again to earth. Or you might read the story there, how, when a Jewish garrison was defending a citadel against overwhelming force, the captain of that small band of defenders, seeing that capture and death were inevitable, cheered his soldiers to fight to the last until death struck them, reminding them that they were only passing away for a time and would return the nobler to earth because of their death for their people. I might bring you on to the time of the Christ Himself, and remind you how, speaking among the Jewish people, He took the doctrine for granted; how, when He spoke of John the Baptist, He reminded His disciples that John the Baptist was Elijah who had come before the coming of the Messiah; how, when He was asked about the blindness of a man, whether it was caused by his own sin or that of his parents, He did not say "How could a man sin before he was born?" as a modern Christian would assert, but answered, taking the possibility of pre-natal sin for granted, that that was not the reason of the blindness of this particular man. So I might lead you on from His time, and from the common belief of the Jews, to the days of the early Church. I might remind you how one Christian father and bishop after another declared the pre-existence of the soul, and how Origen, the greatest and most learned of the teachers of Christian antiquity, declared that every soul received a body according to its deserts and its former actions. It is true, as many of you may know, that the Roman Catholic division of the Church Universal condemned the doctrine at one of its Councils in the seventh century, but it was not a universal condemnation. It condemned the particular form in which Origen had presented it. but guarded itself from a general condemnation. So that there is nothing in the articles of faith of that mighty Communion which makes it against the faith for a Roman Catholic to accept the teaching. You find as you come down the centuries that some of the great sects against which Rome levelled her anathema as heretical—such sects as the Albigenses, of whom Milton wrote one of the most magnificent of his sonnets, had preserved the ancient teaching, and had not permitted it to die. So other sects through the Middle Ages and later preserved the doctrine in their secret teaching. When you come still further down the centuries to the time of Charles II., you find the doctrine again taught in the Anglican Church, not only by the chaplain of the King, but by some of the other clergy of the Church. And I possess an old pamphlet, written by a clergyman of the English Church in that reign, in which he argues that this doctrine of reincarnation is part of the original heritage of Christianity. If you turn from that to the philosophers and the poets, notice how the greatest of them take reincarnation for granted. See how the German poet-philosopher Goethe taught it; how the philosophers Fichte, Lessing, Schopenhauer, follow along the same lines. None of you can be ignorant of Wordsworth's great ode in which he declared:—

"Our birth is but a sleep and a forgetting,
The soul that rises with us, our life's star,
Hath had elsewhere its setting,
And cometh from afar."

So I might point you to other poets, Robert Browning, Dante Gabrielle Rossetti, and many another; for genius has an intuition of truth to which smaller brains may be blind. And coming right down to our own day, let me remind you how Huxley declared that there is nothing in the analogy of Nature against reincarnation, but that there is very much in support of it. I have quoted to you Max Muller's opinion that the greatest philosophers had accepted it, and I ought not to omit from the list of those the sceptical philosopher, Hume, who declared that the doctrine of the pre-existence of the soul was the only doctrine of immortality that a philosopher could look at. To a similar conclusion in our own time came Professor McTaggart, who, after examining and analysing the various theories of immortality, declared that the doctrine of reincarnation was the most rational of them all. So that after all there is nothing to be ashamed of, from the intellectual standpoint, in accepting the doctrine. With such an ancestry we may surely not be too proud at least to examine what it has to say for itself. For the doctrine believed in by Pythagoras and Plato and Virgil and Ovid, and by the mighty host of philosophers through the ages, is surely a doctrine that in the chaos of the modern world deserves to be listened to, whether finally rejected or not.

Now I am only going to put it to you as the most reasonable hypothesis, the most rational of all the theories of human life and death, one out of three possible theories, and the one which best answers the demands of the intellect, explains the difficulties of life, and shows us the reason and the use of death. Now what are the three possible hypotheses? And if two of them are disproved, then the third holds the field until a more rational hypothesis is put forward. That is a very common way, you know, of proving a matter, even in dealing with geometrical problems. Euclid is quite content, when he has destroyed alternative possibilities, to finish up with the comfortable statement that his original proposition is proved.

Now it is rather along that line that I am going. I am not going to pretend to you that I can prove to demonstration this theory of reincarnation. Every one of you must do that for yourselves by the recovery of memory—the final proof. Short of that, I think I can show you it is the most rational of the three. Now the first theory would be the general one of scientific materialism, which does not admit the possibility of a continuing individuality in man; which regards man as coming into the world and going out of it once and for all; which, while it declares the continuity of physical matter, does not acknowledge the continuity of animating intelligence. It regards the one life as all that we have —out of the darkness of birth and into the darkness of death. We shall look into that theory and see how far it explains the difficulties, the problems, which science itself admits; how far it is consistent with human evolution; how far it answers the questions inevitably addressed to science. Then there is the popular Western idea that a soul has a beginning, although it has no end, that it requires a body in order to come into existence, but that when death strikes away the body, it goes on without any further need for it—an idea which makes the everlasting destiny of man depend on the spending of this mortal life, myriads of unending ages to depend on the spending of the life of a few brief and ignorant years. We shall look at that theory also and see how far it satisfies the reason, how far it satisfies the conscience of man; and we shall have to ask how this theory deals with the question of a child living a few hours, a few weeks, or a few months. Does that brief time win for it an everlasting happiness, or by any possibility condemn it to an everlasting torture? Then, having dealt with each of those, we shall come to the theory of reincarnation, and we shall see how it answers the problems that the others leave unsolved, and how we are forced, if we would understand life at all, to accept it. One of the three we must accept—for I know of no other theory of human existence —and we shall see how we are pressed by irrefutable logic to accept the doctrine of the pre-existence of the soul and its independence of the physical body.

Let me take first the scientific view, putting it as clearly as I can. Science, as we know, declares the continuity of matter, one form producing another, and so on and on, and on. The theory which Darwin put to the scientific world tried to connect with the continuity of matter a certain transmission of mental and moral qualities, so that the evolution of consciousness might also be explained. Those of you who were young and vigorous at the time when Darwin's theories convulsed the scientific world will remember how, from his standpoint, mental and moral qualities were transmissible from parents to children. You may remember, if you read much of the literature of the time, how that theory of the transmission of mental and moral qualities was made the basis for future evolution, the foundation of civilisation, the motive for noble living, and how passionately the appeal was made by men like Professor Clifford to live our noblest, our best, and our greatest, so that we might transmit to our children an enriched heritage of mental and moral capacity. But science has travelled far since Darwin published the "Origin of Species," and it has arrived at a conclusion which has knocked to pieces the splendid ethical appeal which was founded on the transmission of mental and moral capacity. No leading scientific man now ventures to declare that mental and moral qualities, acquired during a life, can be transmitted to the offspring. That has been discussed, argued over, controverted, and now the voice of science is clear and definite against it. But even if they could be, it would not help us as much as was once thought. For children are born, in the majority, during the younger time of their parents' life, and the accumulated mental and moral qualities, the wisdom of the old man, the learning acquired during a long life—those are held by their owner after the time for parentage has mostly passed. But that is not the reason, although it is worth thinking over, why this doctrine of transmission has greatly lost its hold. According to that, mental quality, growing, developing, increasing, handed down from parent to child, should show a continual upward path. But it was remarked, and that is one of the things that has undermined the theory, that genius is not transmitted from parent to child. So far from the child of a genius being a genius, he tends to show a mentality rather below the average, not above it. The genius marks the high water mark of the family. After that the family goes down again. Think for a moment; how many men of genius can you remember whose children and grand-children, and great-grand-children are still rising higher and higher in the humanity of our time? None. That is one of the problems that science found so difficult, when talking about man evolving by the transmission of mental capacity from father to child or mother to child. The only case in which you will find persistence for three or four generations of talent is along musical lines. You will find a musical family; you will find that musical family continues perhaps for three generations, and then a genius will be born, and after that the faculty disappears. But that does not look so much like transmission, as it looks like Nature preparing a body for a genius, with the nervous organism which is necessary for the full showing out of the artistic power. It looks rather as though that family, talented in music, prepared a physical organism with delicate nerves, with sensitive ear, and sensitive fingers, and that when that family organism was ready the genius stepped in to take it, and then the use of the family was over, and it went down again to be lost among the ordinary humanity of its time. For these, and many other reasons, Darwin's theory has been given up. Science goes further than giving up the theory; science has struck the death note of humanity as to high increase of mental ability, if it is to be transmitted, by declaring that genius tends to be sterile; and the lower the mental type the more rapid the reproduction and multiplication. Now of that there is practically no doubt in the scientific world to-day. But how are you going to deal with that, side by side with evolution? If the theory as to the more intellectual be that they produce a smaller number of offspring, what hope is there for the raising of humanity to loftier realms of mental power where the majority are concerned? And remember that the fate of the majority is the most important for the race. It is not enough to have a few flowers of genius, if the intellectual level of humanity does not rise millennium after millennium.

Let us pass from that point of the scientific view and take another scientific difficulty. Human evolution is marked not only by mental, but by moral growth; and the moral is even more important than the mental. Man is gradually learning to substitute the sense of duty and obligation for the enforcement by physical strength; man is slowly learning to substitute compassion for cruelty, the helping of the weak, the sick, and the miserable, instead of the casting of them out to perish, careless of what suffering they may undergo. It is the boast of civilised nations that they guard the weak, nurse the sick, comfort the afflicted. But how have those qualities that make men human evolved in the struggle for existence? The struggle for existence is the very opposite; the fittest survive. But who are the "fit" to survive in the struggle? Not the gentle, the compassionate, the tender, and the self-sacrificing, but the unscrupulous, and the brutal, the strong, and the man without conscience or care for the weaker. That is where your difficulty comes in. Huxley saw it, and Huxley declared, in the words of a Master, that the law of the survival of the fittest is the law of the evolution of the brute, but the law of self-sacrifice is the law of the evolution of the man. That is true. But then, if Darwin's theory were true, those who sacrifice themselves would be the very ones most valuable for the handing on of their nobler and more human qualities. Now, mother-love, one of the most splendid of qualities, evolves in the brute and evolves in humanity. But the mother, who sacrifices herself for her children,, perishes in the struggle, and the children are left uncared for. In the animal kingdom, in the fierce fight for life, mother-love is a disadvantage. The lioness is shot by the hunter when she endeavours to defend her cubs, and then the cubs perish from hunger. The bird that trails along with apparently broken wing, in order to lure away the hunter from her nest and her nestlings, is likely to be shot, and the young ones die. How, then, can mother-love be evolved in the fierce struggle? How can it be handed on, even if handing on were possible? And here is one of the problems that science cannot answer; how are social qualities evolved, as they lead to the destruction of those who show them out most plainly? When science comes to answer that question, it finds itself facing a dead wall. But even that is not the most hopeless side. Supposing science in this matter is right; supposing materialistic science is right in saying that we have no past and no hereafter, but only the little span between the cradle and the grave. What sort of hope in that is to be found for the vast masses of the hopeless population of the world? Is it any comfort to the man rotting in a slum to tell him that this is the only experience of the world that he shall have? What can that doctrine do for him save drive him into recklessness and brutality in order to get the little pleasure he can out of the brief span of life which is his only experience of the world. I do not say that that disproves the doctrine; it does not. But it is a doctrine of despair to man; and we should want clear proof before we could accept it. If it be true, as science says, that "nature is stronger than nurture," the nature you bring with you into the world is stronger than anything you can do to train the child. Now that is true; but if that be so, then what of the myriads of those who are born congenital criminals, hopeless idiots, or even stupid, in a world where craft and strength are inexorable? If it be true, it is the saddest news humanity has ever had. It would mean hopelessness for the masses, and hope only for the few who happen to be at the time, whether by wealth or genius, or power of arms, or power of brain, objects of envy to every one, unjustly possessing all the joy of earth where others are miserable, poor, and helpless.

Now let us see whether the popular religious doctrine is satisfactory to reason and morality. What is that doctrine, briefly stated? It is this: that every soul is new created; that is the first point to get clearly in mind. But when the soul comes into the body prepared for it, it brings a character with it. Where did it get it? If new created, then the character of the new-born child is imprinted upon it by its Creator. From that position there is no escape. Now, many children are born criminals, and cannot be anything else through the whole of their life. Many are born diseased, and disease distorts their thought and dwarfs their powers. Many are born deformed, miserable. Many are born vicious. Who, under these conditions, is responsible for all these? Then other people are born just the opposite—clever, healthy, with everything in their favour. Are they also new created souls? And if one can be created noble and pure in character, where lies the justice in regard to those who are born criminal, vicious, and diseased? But let us take it that it is so for the moment; the new created soul comes either saint or criminal into the world. Follow them on through the whole of life, and what very different, what startlingly contrasting destinies life brings them. Do not take a criminal at first; let us take a decent peasant, born in some country village, and leading a laborious and industrious life. Even in such a case as that, honourable and upright as he is, how little that man has of all that the world can give. I do not mean of money, luxury, and comfort; but I mean of the faculty to understand; of the power to enjoy the nobler things of earth. To that peasant the sunset only means that there will be rain to-morrow or fine weather; to that man the beauty of cloud and sky only means the effect upon his crops. That man knows nothing of the joy of the artist, of the splendour of colour, of the artistic delight in all the exquisite beauty of nature. For him the hedge with its garlands of wild rose and honeysuckle only means "green stuff" that gets in the way of the sun, which otherwise would shine upon his corn and make it grow better. Why should he be deprived of all that the artist enjoys? why should life be so narrow to him and so wide to some others? Is that all he is to have of life? Is the artist or the genius the better for his wider experience of life? If so, and there is only one life for all, those are robbed everlastingly of a bliss they might have had, and no ages in heaven will make up for the paucity and poverty of the intellectual and artistic life on earth. You cannot balance up things that way. Either this life is useful, or it does not matter. If it is useful, that handicapped man will always be behind in the race, always less well off than the other. If it is not useful, then why should we be plunged into this world at all, to have the trouble of a physical existence, unless it is to teach us a lesson of priceless value and of enduring worth? And what about that babe I spoke of, who only comes in for a few hours of life? What happens to it on the other side of death? If he gets salvation for nothing, then it is rather hard on the people who have to live 70, 80, or 90 years, whose lives are full of trouble, difficulty, and suffering. In these, I am only taking ordinary cases that you see around you on every side. May I take two extreme cases and show you how this theory of life works out? I do not know your city, and I do not know whether you have here the slums that we have in the older countries, or whether here in your back streets you have such places as I know existed in London, when I was a member of the School Board for the poorest London district in the East End. I do not know whether such slums exist here as I have been to in Paris, behind and beyond the splendour and glitter of Parisian life; or such slums as I have seen in Sheffield, Glasgow, Edinburgh, and Manchester. Supposing you came with me one day on one of my school board journeys, and supposing I took you down Whitechapel Road, and then down one of the little roads that turn off it, and then into a filthy court in which that road ends. The whole place is covered with rotting vegetables and with filthy fragments of food. I take you down into a cellar where there is no light and no air. No air or sun can get there save through the trap-door, which opens up into the street. A woman is lying there, and she has just given birth to a child. The child is not wanted; the mother is not glad that she is the mother of the boy; she only looks on him as an added burden, a new trouble in a miserable life; she is only a harlot out of the streets. The father—who knows? some drunken sailor, some thief, some miserable vagabond tramping the streets, who can tell? There is the child. Go and look at it. Look at the face; look at the shape of the head; see how the forehead is shaped. Why, there is no forehead; the head goes back from the top of the eyebrows. There is no room there for the instrument of the mind, no place, physically, for intellectual capacities to use as their organ. There is plenty of room at the back of the head for the passions and appetites of the brute. The sociologist who looks at the child says: "Oh, yes, he is a congenital criminal; he will grow up and die a criminal, and you cannot do anything with him; he has brought that with him into the world."

Who made him? Who is responsible for him? Who threw him into that filthy cellar of a London Court? He is going to live in spite of his misery. Nobody helps him to live. He is brought up on blows, not on kisses like happier children. When he is a child of three or four, put your hand out to him as you pass and he shrinks back and puts up his arms or hands as defence. He thinks it is a blow you are going to give him, for no hand is stretched out to him save to give him a blow. He will tell you a lie. If he does not tell lies he gets beaten. He will try to pick your pocket. If he goes home without some stolen thing, to the cellar he calls "home," he will be thrashed and sent to bed without supper. He is taught to steal and lie, as you teach your children to be honest and to tell the truth. His little lips use the foulest language. He hears nothing else. Horrible, profane, and filthy words come out from those child-lips. He knows no better, he means nothing by them. It is the language he hears all around him every day and every night. Presently the policeman gets hold of him, brings him before the magistrate. Sometimes so little is he that his head will not come above the bar of the dock, and he has to be put on a stool or a chair so that the judge, who is going to sentence him, can see the child. He is thrown into gaol. He comes out after a few days worse than he went in. Over and over again the same story is told. Back he goes to gaol, until at last he becomes an habitual criminal. What else could he be? He has never had a chance of being anything else. The law to him is enemy; society to him is foe; his hand is against everybody because everybody's hand is against him. And so on he goes from bad to worse; sentence after sentence, degradation after degradation, and at last that miserable creature strikes a blow in anger, as many a blow has been struck at him all his miserable life, and the blow kills. He is arrested for the last time, and for the last time he is tried, and for the last time he is sentenced; and he goes from the dock to the condemned cell, and from the condemned cell to the gallows, and from the gallows to the quicklime of the criminal's grave in the prison yard; and then? dare you say that that man will have a future of everlasting misery when his earth life has been misery from cradle to gallows? What justice is there in that? The child brought the criminal tendency with him, and no one ever helped him out of it. He is a victim, not a criminal; he is a helpless straw on the stream of a hopeless destiny. He is not fit for heaven—there is no doubt about that. It is not right to send him to hell. What will you do with him? There is no place for him in the world. Earth had no place for him. Heaven has no room for him. Hell would be an added cruelty to the cruelty that he has already suffered. What will you do with him? whither shall he go? And it is not as though nobody else could be made on a better pattern; because you may have the soul of a genius born, and everything may be as easy for him as crime was easy for the other. This genius is born in the happy environment of a happy home, father and mother coaxing him on to everything that is good and noble, checking the wrong with kindness and encouraging the good with love. The child goes to the best school the country can give him; from school he goes to the University. He takes prize after prize, medal after medal, honour after honour, till he goes out into the world with mind glad and happy and gay with the beauty and the splendour of the life that is opening up before him. He possesses talents that make him the glory of his nation; power that makes him the idol of the populace. He writes, he paints. Whatever may be the line of his genius, it is a joy to practice it and not a labour, and the creative power in him embodies itself in some deathless work of art which makes his name immortal in the history of the world. And so he goes on from one gladness to another, from one joy to another; and the world is the better because that man has lived. Nations are happier because of his power; he has added to the beauty and the gladness of the world; and when, after a long life, he dies, a whole nation laments him. The attendants at his funeral are the messengers of kings and the greatest of the nation, and they bury him, say, in Westminster Abbey, and write his name up high in the history of the time and all men praise him. But what else could he have been? He brought the power with him; circumstances guarded and helped him. His life was as much foredoomed to fame as the other was fore-doomed to infamy. Who is going to make it even be-tween those two men? Where is justice if neither de-served his fate, if the one was branded criminal without desert, and the other has genius without desert? Those are the problems that men and women have to face. It is not enough to tell us: "Who art thou, O man, that repliest against God?" For God gave the reason which demands the question, and God gave the conscience which is not satisfied with the injustice of life. And I defy thoughtful men and women to accept that view when once they think it out. They accept it because they do not think, not because they do.

But now let us ask whether there is any other view of life which will make these things intelligible. I can tell you in three or four sentences the theory of reincarnation:—That every man is a living spirit; he is part of the life of the Supreme, he is the offspring of Deity; as sparks come forth from a fire, so comes he forth from the Divine Spirit. He comes to earth to learn. All are equally ignorant when plunged into human life. Ignorance is the only original sin, and it is not criminal but inevitable. As the powers of the Deity within him are unfolded, he grows into the stature of the Perfect Man. Passing out of the first human life, ignorant, helpless, having committed what we should call crimes—but which were no crimes to that new soul, without knowledge to distinguish between good and evil, but were only experiences—the man passes into the intermediate world of which I was speaking the other night. There he learns that these things are not the best to do, because they bring trouble on the other side. The subject who is murdered meets there the man who has murdered. The one hates the other and makes his life there miserable. The murderer takes his cravings and his passions with him; he is tormented by them on the other side until they are worn out—starved out—and then he passes on to a higher world where everything in him of good is nourished and increases; then back to earth he comes again with the gained experience and the added knowledge to learn other lessons here, to pass on again and reap the fruit of this learning; to pass on into the heavenly world and weave experience into faculty, and with that added faculty to come back once more; and so on and on life after life in this great cycle of births and deaths, every life adding some necessary experience, every re-birth bringing with it larger and wider powers, learning righteousness by the suffering that treads on the heels of evil, learning compassion by the sorrow which is endured under the yoke of oppression, learning all lessons by experience and transmuting them into character, until perfection is reached, until the perfect man shines out in all the splendour of man become divine. Then compulsory reincarnation is over, and unless the man returns as Saviour he passes on, all earth's lessons learnt, into wider life and more splendid opportunities.

Now, that is the theory. Let us try to apply it to

human life; take a savage; that savage, for example, may be one of your aboriginal inhabitants here whom Darwin has put on record. The savage does not know what we call good and evil, he does not know what we call right and wrong. The savage is hungry, no food is convenient, but he has a wife. He kills his wife and turns her into his dinner. A missionary comes along and he says: "You should not have done that, that is very wrong." The savage does not know what is meant by wrong, and when the missionary argues that it is not good to kill the wife, he answers, feeling quite comfortable after the good meal, "I assure you she was very good." Now I have only read that story out of Darwin; he has put it on record. What are you going to do with a man like that? He has not yet learned what good means, except the satisfaction of a physical craving. That man has not got in him anything that answers to your appeal. Education means drawing out what is in a man, but there is nothing in this man to draw out in response to a moral appeal. But take one of your children. If you were to say to him: "It is wrong for a man to eat a man," the child would say: "Oh yes, father, of course it is." You have not got to argue it. The child would say, "I know it is wrong." There is something in him that tells him that that is so. There is something in the child that answers when you tell him that it is not right for man to kill man. What makes the difference between him and the savage? We say growth; that the child's soul has had many experiences behind it of murders and robberies, and of all the results that flow out of them, and in the life beyond death has had imprinted on the memory of the spirit the results which grow out of the experiences of human life. All your children, when they are brought into the world, are born with certain ideas or tendencies to think in a particular direction, and as soon as education reaches them the tendency at once asserts itself; but the tendency is only there because of past experience; you cannot obtain an answer from a soul that has not brought with it the characteristics. A few years ago I came across the story of a child of a North American Indian. Her whole tribe had been wiped out by a neighbouring tribe, and a kindly missionary woman, going through the burnt huts and the ruins of the village, heard the cry of the little child, and she hunted for the child amongst the debris and charred remains and found a baby girl. She took the child back with her and brought it up in her own home. At first the child was quick, intelligent, and answered to what she was taught. But at about the age of 8 or 9 years her teacher came to a dead wall, she could not teach her any more. There was no further answer. She could not teach her the commonest moral ideas; she could not teach her not to steal, she could not teach her not to lie. And this good lady, who was an earnest Christian, was broken-hearted because she could not understand what this little child was who could not learn such a common truth. The child could not learn it because behind her there was not the experience which had taught it, and you cannot draw out of a child what is not in it. That was what my scientific friend, Buchner, meant by saying that "nature is stronger than nurture." You can mould and shape if you have something to mould and shape; but where there is a total absence of the moral sense all your moral appeals fall useless and the child cannot understand. But that only means that it is young; there is no need to break your heart over it as though it were some monstrous creature doomed to misery; it is only a baby soul that has not yet learnt enough to answer to the instruction of the teacher. From this standpoint, then, the criminal is the young ego, or soul, if you prefer the word, not to be despised, not to be hated, not to be trampled upon, but to be taught, disciplined, and built into a little better type than the type he brought with him into the world. I know it would turn your criminology up-side-down, for you would have to deal with your criminals in a very different way from that in which you deal with them now. You would have to understand a principle which I see you have just—for the first time, so far as I know—introduced here: the indeterminate sentence. Now I do not know how you are working that, but it is a right principle. It is the principle that sends a man to a hospital till he is cured. You do not send a man to a hospital for seven days for small-pox, and then let him go out and scatter the disease all about; and you should not send your morally diseased man to a prison for a term, and then set him loose again to prey upon society. Only, of course, you have to change your present treatment. It must not be punitive in the sense it often is; no dark cells, no bread and water, no lash. Those are not the ways to train. What you need is the teacher, the man who will help and train the idle man to labour; train the useless man to a trade. A very good rule is this, that if the man will not work neither shall he eat. Let the criminal earn his dinner before he gets it, for the criminal ought not to be better off than the honest workman. A criminal should not be kept idle and useless, a burden on the earnings of the honest and industrious labourer. The criminal should keep himself, support himself; but prison products should not be sold outside at a lower price, underselling those of honest labour. You will have to change your prison principles, I know, but you would train up men who, when they went through the gateway of death, would have learnt something by their contact with civilised society; they would not be tossed out by the gallows because earth cannot manage them; they would be kept as children are kept in a home, to be trained and disciplined until fit for freedom and citizenship. That is a very different treatment to that adopted nowadays, but it is a treatment that will inevitably grow out of the recognition of the fact that the criminal is only a tiresome child, a savage born into civilised society, a kind of anachronism who should learn his lessons the better because he has come among people more evolved, and whose birth into a civilised nation should be a blessing to him instead of the curse that it is at the present time.

Then you come to the genius. What is he? He is the soul which has gone through life after life, and has gradually gathered together and accumulated all the results of life's experience until at last he has reached the splendour that we call genius. He has earned it. It is no gift to him, which would imply injustice. It is the fairly-earned wages of lives of toil and struggle. That is what reincarnation means—fair payment all round. But do not confuse the fair payment, as some do, by thinking that wealth or position is necessarily the result of virtue. It is not. You may have a very bad character, and yet you may possess a great fortune. You cannot pay virtue with gold. The payment of virtue is being virtuous, not so much balance in your bank. You must realise that, or else you will never understand the world. What wealth means is this: that the man who now has it earned it by strong desire and by spreading happiness amongst other people when he was here before. But if, in the possession of it, he has a bad and selfish character, it means that his character before was selfish, and that the happiness he spread was for his own ends, and not for the sake of those he helped. Now, of course, bribery is against the law, but in the old country a man may spend £50,000 on an election; when he has done that a good many times, he has made a claim on his party, and when the party comes into power it may give him a title. If he has given a park to the poor town, he is all the more sure of being called "My Lord." Now, what is the moral value of the man? He has spent his money and he has given the park merely to buy for himself a title—selfish right through. None the less, the park makes thousands of poor people happier and healthier than they were, and the man reaps as he sowed: his selfish motive works out in selfish character, and nature gives him back the physical happiness which he spread amongst thousands of the poor. Nature is absolutely just. Nature gives a man exactly what he earns. A good chemist may beat his wife, but he will not fail in his chemical experiments because he is a wife-beater. Nor will a very good husband make a great chemical discovery if he knows nothing of chemical law. You must try to understand the perfect justice of nature, which is the expression of God; His justice and not topsy-turvydom. Exactly what a man sows he reaps, and by that law he grows to genius and to sainthood. The child who is born a saint—that is the result of lives of effort and self-denial. It is no free gift given to that child. His saintly character has been wrought in the furnace of pain. That was why Edward Carpenter wrote, catching a glimpse of this same truth, and speaking of a man wrestling with Satan, and losing his body time after time in the long struggle: "Every pain that I suffered in one body became a power that I wielded in the next." That is the result of reincarnation. Whatever you sow comes back to you, and you take your choice of the seed that you are pleased to sow. What it means for all of you is this; that you can become exactly what you like. You may have a small talent to-day, a little talent, say, for music. You know you cannot be a musical genius in this life. Never mind; go on practising steadily, do your best; you will have time after time to come back greater and greater, until the talent becomes genius and you reach the zenith of your aspirations. There are some people who cannot be happy while others are miserable around them, some who are not satisfied with what the world gives them when they see others who are in suffering and misery, whose aspirations are thwarted, whose work is not as great as their will. Never mind; work on, hope on, aspire on. That work, those aspirations and those efforts will come back to you in the heavenly world, to be changed into power and capacity and ability to serve. This is the teaching of eternal hope. Chance after chance is given you in life. You have failed? Never mind; it is only one day out of many days. The failure now means conquest to-morrow, and the wisdom learned by mistakes is yours for ever. It would be very hard if you had only one experience and your life were a failure. But what does it matter when life after life is yours, when in the end all your grandest hopes will be inevitably realised? The sooner, if you work, the more quickly if you throw all your thought, heart and soul into your life. You can be whatever you determine to be, for you are Divine. That is what reincarnation means. The worst criminal, the highest saint—they have one life, one spirit, equal possibilities. The only difference is that the saint came into the world ages ago, and has been growing up ever since; whilst the criminal came into the world but a life or two ago, and has still to tread the same long road the saint has already trodden.

And to those of you who are Christian men and women, who regard the words of your great Teacher as words of truth—what did He say to you? This: "Be ye therefore perfect, as your Father in Heaven is perfect." But you cannot be that in one brief life. Your weakness cannot blossom into divine strength before the grave closes over you, nor your ignorance into divine wisdom. But He who spoke knew that there was time enough, knew that you could grow from strength to strength, knew that Divine perfection is your destiny, and urged you to step forward on the road that leads thereto. The words would be but mockery, if you had only a single life. The words are a splendid inspiration, if you know that growth is possible and time is yours. Oh, if I could tell you what it was to come out of all the struggle and misery in London, and to know that it was not hopeless, and that those miserable drunken men and women, those children of wretchedness and vice, were only babes in the beginning of their life, and that they would have chance after chance, life after life, growth ever continuing, unfolding to absolute perfection, and that one could help them in the upward climb, quicken their progress, inspire them with hope; that one could say to the criminal: "My brother, where you are I was myself; I have grown to where I am, you shall do the same; and as for the saints above us, we shall both grow up to take our stand where they now stand in the eternal life." And if you knew how the heart of the miserable responds to it, how the depraved and wretched spring up to the idea! To tell them they have other chances, to tell them they shall have other opportunities, that there is nothing in all the splendour of nature that does not belong of right to every man—that is to carry light into the darkness and to make them feel that they themselves are Divine.

Such, then, is the teaching of reincarnation. Compare it with the other two theories of life, and judge you as you will. It is not mine to tell you what you ought to believe; not mine to try to impose upon you anything that I myself may think or know to be true. The duty of the lecturer is only to point out the way and to let people walk that way on their own feet, not carried in the arms of another's thought. Read, study, think for yourself, and apply this key to the turning of the locks of human misery and human ignorance. If you do, you will gradually see that it is true. If you study, you will come to understand its far-reaching importance; and what I have said to you is only as a synopsis showing you where to study, the lines along which you may carry on your own investigation; then it will be to you what it has been to thousands of us, the chasing away of darkness, the dawn of light in the world, the rising of the sun in which every child of man shall rejoice for ever. Sin is the ignorance of childhood; sanctity is the crown of manhood; and so, on and on, until every child of man shall have grown to the fulness of the stature of the Christ.

Life after Death

One of the quaintest things in the great play of Hamlet is the fact that in a very early part of it the statement is made as to death that it is the bourne from which no traveller returns, and then the whole of the play is built up towards the final demonstration of a murder of which the ghost, returning from that same bourne, was originally the revealer. That sort of inconsistency as regards belief in a life after death, the possibility of communicating with other worlds, the general doubtfulness and vagueness of men's opinions on the subject, seems to spread through the whole of our modern life. Despite the fact that it is sometimes alleged that Christianity has made the after-death life more certain than any other religion, you find a far greater vagueness amongst Christian nations than you do among the non-Christian people either of ancient or of modern times. In Rome, as many of you know, people were quite willing to lend money on security which was valid on the other side of death, and I suppose the absolute belief in the persistence of human personality could hardly be given a more definite proof than that. You find among many nations of the world an utter contempt of death. You find the Hindu wife who will not re-marry as a widow because she does not regard death as in any sense severing the marriage tie. From her standpoint the marriage of a widow is simply a case of bigamy. And so in other nations also you find this definite realisation of a super-physical life, and of the fact that men and women on the other side of death remain the same persons that they were on this side, with the same emotions and the same affections, the same ties, the same obligations to each other.

Now, why is it that in modern days, among the most civilised peoples, who boast so much of their religion as giving certainty of life on the other side of death, why is it that among ourselves the practical belief in that after-death life has become so little potent on conduct? Why is it so vague and so indeterminate? Why—testing it by what is the fairest test, that the proof of the reality of a belief is its effect on conduct—is it that the belief in an after-death life has become so very feeble among ourselves? I think that the chief reason for this has been the want of reason in the views taken of the after-death life through many a century of Christian teaching. The idea that the endless ages of everlasting life were determined once for all by the passing, and often trivial, events of the brief life between cradle and grave, I think has had much to do towards making the vision of the other life unreal in our minds. It was not so some centuries ago. Many of you will remember when the preachers of Christendom, dilating on the joys of heaven and the terrors of hell, used many a metaphor and many a description that would be rejected either with disgust or laughter now, according to the minds of the people who happened to hear it. Recall as an instance of what

I am putting a famous description in one of the most eloquent of the great writers, or, rather, preachers, of the Calvinists. He traced out his idea of the everlasting nature of hell, and he described a huge mountain made up of grains of sand, vast, immense. He bade his hearers imagine that if a bird once in a thousand years came and carried away one grain of sand in its bill, that then, in the immeasurable ages which it would take to exhaust that mountain grain by grain, during the whole of that time the misery of hell would have been continuing, and would be no nearer to its ending than when the first grain of sand was carried away. Now one cannot wonder that against a doctrine so horrible the reason and the conscience of men rose up in revolt; and the very fact that it is so, the very fact that no such sermon would be preached now, to a congregation of educated people, at least, shows you that the old teaching has lost its hold, and men have been left vague and indeterminate, knowing not how to replace the teaching they were unable to believe. The whole thing was out of relation. No man felt himself bad enough for an everlasting hell; none good enough for an everlasting heaven. Hence the feeling that it was not rational has gradually weakened any idea of the after-death life in men's minds, and many, perhaps most, men of the world will now say: " Well, we cannot know anything about it. We must do our best here, and hope that it will be all right on the other side." That is the common thing that you hear now from men and women, decent-living, thoughtful men and women, but unable to substitute for a belief they had rejected any rational conception of a life on the other side of death.

Now is it possible that we should know anything about that other life? Is it possible to discover the facts which we shall all have to face, for the one thing that is absolutely certain for everyone of us is the fact of death. It is the one thing we cannot escape from, the one destiny of which we are absolutely sure. In these modern days, as in the elder days, it is reasserted that some knowledge is possible—knowledge of those worlds which may be gained as we gain knowledge of foreign lands, by travelling therein and observing what there may be seen. There are two ways, especially, offered to the modern world: one easy, but not very satisfactory; the other difficult, but growing more and more satisfactory the more we know of it; the way which is put forward by our friends who are called the Spiritualists, and that which is put forward by those who call themselves Theosophists.

Now let us look at those two ways and see, just for a moment, how they differ, before I go on to try and explain to you clearly the methods of theosophical investigation and the results that have come by the use of those methods.

The Spiritualistic way, I said, was comparatively easy. It does not demand from those who would learn about it any special way of living, any special kind of study. It is done *for* people, not *by* them, and done by a certain class of people, who, by a peculiarity of their physical constitution, are able to act as links between this world and the world beyond, being what is called mediums, mediums of communication. The method of communication lies either in a person leaving his body and allowing someone else to occupy it, or by the definite materialisation of this discarnate entity reappearing in the world that he has left. Now as to the first of those methods, the stepping out of the body and the occupation of the body by someone else, there is an enormous amount of evidence, not only Spiritualistic, but scientific also, to show that more than one personality can utilise a human body. The cases of multiple personality, which are now being so much studied by psychologists, form a remarkable and interesting contribution to the knowledge as to the ways in which the human body may be tenanted, and the fact that not one entity only may possibly occupy one human body. But even taking that for granted and accepting it, there is so much spiritualistic evidence for such possession by discarnate entities that no one who has gone carefully into it can pretend that all the phenomena can be fraudulent, even though some of them have been so; those who have studied the subject carefully and long know that, when you have made every possible allowance for fraud, there is an irreducible minimum of phenomena which nothing can possibly destroy. I am not myself a Spiritualist, but I deem it right to bear witness to the work that has been done by that large body in establishing the survival of human personality on the other side of death, against ridicule and threat, against police prosecution, and every other weapon that ignorance could use. That body of men and women has gone on steadily accumulating evidence, until numbers of the leading Scientists of the world now admit what for so many years they denied. To their courage these proofs are due. Still, if a man be an utter Materialist who cannot be convinced, save by an appeal to the senses, then I know of no better evidence than can be gained by a careful and scientific investigation into Spiritualistic phenomena. My objection to them does not lie then on the ground that they are always unreliable, but rather on this ground, that the people from the other side with whom you come into touch along these lines are very rarely those who can give a full and reliable statement. They are mostly those who are nearest to the earth that they have left. Not quite always, but in the great majority of cases they do not show signs of high intelligence nor of a wide knowledge of the conditions of life on the other side of death. Their statements, while sometimes interesting, are not full and detailed, save in one or two cases which stand out from the rest of the teachings. I look on the contributions of Spiritualism to a knowledge of the after-death life as very limited in their character, although convincing as to the fact of survival on the other side. Our objections also lie partly along the lines of the depletion of human vitality, the injury to the mediums themselves, which so constantly accompanies these investigations. Were there none other, then I think we should be justified in following them, but if there be a better and a surer way, that is the way that I would rather commend to your attention, and I believe that there is. It is the way in which man may utilise his own spiritual nature in coming into touch with those who have cast off the burden of the flesh. If on the other side of death you are spirits, you are spirits quite as much on this side also. If your spiritual nature is capable of communicating from that world to this, the same spiritual nature is capable of going out from this world and investigating the other, while still we can return to this. That is the line which the great teachers of the past have followed. That is the line which the religions of the past and present have recognised in their own greatest teachers, in those who have come as the teachers of religion to men. Based as it is on the same Spiritual nature in all of us, it rests on us to utilise it and to make investigations for ourselves. It turns on the fact that you are spirits encased in bodies, that those bodies are now in touch with other worlds as well as with the physical, as I was pointing out to you the other night, and that it is possible so to train your physical and your psychical bodies as to work as a living intelligence in the psychical body as well as in the physical, and so for yourselves to investigate the worlds that lie on the other side of death. Now it is along that line that Theosophical investigation has gone. A person, being a living spiritual intelligence, need not wait to know what is on the other side until death strikes away his body and releases him from the present house of the physical frame. This body of ours is meant to be a dwelling, but not a prison, and the key of it should be in our own hands and not only in the hands of death. That is the fact that has been so often proclaimed, so often verified, and in what I am going to lay before you now, it is on those investigations that I shall entirely base all that I say. I do not propose to go beyond the facts that I can myself say I have verified as being true, for it is our habit amongst ourselves to verify over and over again what anyone may have observed, and so gradually to bring a consensus of testimony to establish the facts as to the other worlds.

I start, then, with the statement that it is possible to leave the body and return to it. You may say: "But that sounds very curious," and yet you are doing it every night of your lives. Whenever you go to sleep you, as a living intelligence, leave your body, and that leaving of the body in sleep, at least, is a fact that is being more and more recognised by scientific investigators who utilise what is called trance, which is only a form of sleep, a form of sleep in which for the time the physical body is insensitive to stimulus, but fundamentally the same as the sleep state. Now it is proved beyond possibility of contradiction that such leaving of the body is possible, that under these conditions, as I was pointing out to you the other night, the living intelligence is very much more active and potent than when it is within the normal physical conditions. And it is on those facts that we start in our investigations, the possibility of leaving the physical body without loss of intelligence. It is not, however, on the ordinary dream state that we depend, but on the deliberate leaving of the body that comes by training yourself, in the sleep state as well as in the waking, until you have bridged the loss of consciousness between the two, can leave the body without loss of consciousness, and bring back and imprint on the brain that which outside the body you have observed. Then when you have accomplished that, you can go a step further, opening up these inner psychical senses. It becomes, after a time, unnecessary to leave the physical body while you are exercising the higher senses. You learn gradually to unfold these so that they are under your control, so that you can observe the next world while living in the waking consciousness here. You must remember the next world is not far away. It is around you all the time. Your friends who have thrown off the body do not travel far away to some distant country, but remain near those they love, and are visible to the opened eyes which can see the finer matter in which then the intelligence is clothed. I say then, that you all have bodies of that finer matter, and in those bodies the senses whereby these bodies may also be seen; and if that line be followed and practised, then, while wide awake to the things of this world, you can examine also the things of the world that we call the other side of death, but which is really the world that is around us all the time, the world whose inhabitants are with us wherever we may be, the world which thus becomes a world of knowledge, and not only a world in whose reality we hope.

Now let us see what is happening when a person is throwing off the physical body, the moment of death. Exactly the same thing happens then as happens to every one of you each night as you fall asleep. There is no pain in the moment of death, no agony in the passing out of the body, even where signs of physical suffering are. The suffering is over, although there may be some touch of action in the physical body which stimulates the suffering no longer felt. The intelligence, passing out, does not feel the last contortions of the dying body, but is turned in, as it were, within its own immortal existence, conscious of the world that is opening around it, and conscious of the world it is leaving for the last time. Hence those who gather round a death-bed should be careful that, in the wrench of the parting to them, the friend who is going onwards is not disturbed by any noisy demonstrations of sorrow which may check his peaceful passing and recall his thought for a moment to the pain on earth. Most religions have wisely appointed prayers for the dying, more for the sake of the calm of the living than for the sake of the intelligence passing on into the next world. It is true that these prayers for the dying, as prayers for the dead, are the messages of love to the passing one, that ought never to be forgotten nor omitted. For there is really no death, nothing that is a ceasing of life is possible, and there is no reason why you should not love and pray for your friends on the other side of death as much as you have done while they were still with you, for, though invisible, they have not passed out of reach. Now for about six and thirty hours after the actual moment of death a man stays in a condition of happy but dreamy consciousness. I mean by that, he is not conscious of anything around him, neither in this world nor on the other side, wrapped rather in what you would call dreams—the weariness of the sickness over, perfectly comfortable, happy and content. There is that pause between this world and the next lasting for this brief space of mortal hours. After that, different will be the experiences of the one who has passed on according to the life which has closed upon earth. The easiest way to make this clear is to classify, however roughly, those who pass on. Take the lowest human type, the savage, the congenital criminal, the man of very violent uncontrolled passions, the man whose only enjoyments here have been in the gratification of the appetites of the body. You have there a great class of human beings whose experiences—and there is no object in hiding it—are of a painful and distressing kind. It could not be otherwise, if you think for a moment, in a world where law is changeless and where the effect follows the cause in inviolable sequence. What could happen to a man all of whose pleasures are connected with the physical world, when the physical body is struck away from him by death, when all the passions remain, but gratification is no longer possible? What can happen save a painful craving for the banished pleasures, a suffering from the desires that no longer can be gratified, a passionate desire again to feel the feelings which on earth represented the only form of happiness he knew, and an equally great disappointment and frustration when he finds that those pleasures are now beyond his grasp? That is what all the stories of the different hells of different religions have been built upon, but by their exaggeration they have destroyed their utility. Law is Law. The drunkard and the profligate, victims of insatiable desires, must inevitably suffer on the other side of death until those desires are worn out by literal starvation by the lack of the food which in the physical body could be supplied. It is no punishment inflicted, it is an inevitable sequence; no arbitrary penalty of an angry God, but the working out of that most merciful though just law of nature, that a man shall reap according to his sowing, and by the reaping of the harvest shall learn the wisdom or unwisdom of the planting of the seed.

There comes out the difference between the endless and the temporary hell, for I do not mind if you choose to use the word. Suffering in a world of law is remedial. By suffering, nature teaches us the things that we ought not to do. The things that injure us, physically, morally, mentally, they are all accompanied by suffering, whether in this world or any other. The profligate, though he may gain pleasure for a time, pays the price of that pleasure in his ruined nerves, in his shattered body, even in this life, and on this side of the grave. So, on the other side, he reaps the similar penalty of continuing desires that he cannot gratify. But the moment that the desires are exhausted, he passes onwards free from the suffering that he made for himself, and the scourge of his vices, created by himself, ceases to give him pain when the vice is exhausted by disuse. There it is that the man learns the lesson that it is an evil thing to lead the passion-life of the brute when grown into human form. There he learns his earliest lessons, that it is not worth while to be the slave of his vices, of his passions. He is forced to conquer them by the conditions around him, and he grows in knowledge by the inevitable sequence of pain. Others you may find there also of brutal and violent character, always learning a lesson which on earth they refused to learn; and you find in some of the old religions, where these facts were well known, that the ordering of the man's life here was made so that he might not suffer there, and in the ordering of the man's life, men were always recommended and commanded to give up, after they reach old age, the ordinary pleasures of the world, to turn more to thought than to physical pleasures, more to study, meditation, and prayer than to worldly interests, preparing for themselves deliberately things that they can carry on to the other side, so that, passing through death, they might have left their passions behind them, and have carried on pure emotions and noble thoughts.

Now after that stage of the after-death life, a stage which is a stage of suffering, there is one possibility that might well be avoided, which sometimes causes suffering at the present time. Thought on that side is much more powerful than it is here, and the things that you believe on this side are forms and forces that you meet with on the next. That is the real mischief now of the preaching, in some of the narrower forms of Christianity, of that old doctrine of everlasting suffering. It causes terror on the other side. It creates occasionally for those victims some hours or days of suffering, partly due to terror, partly due to the manufacture of the very horrors that they dread. One of the experiences that some of us have had in going about among the people on the other side has been the finding occasionally of some unlearned but earnest Christian who has believed in that terrible doctrine of hell, while still he was living here. We have found him in a state of terror, afraid of a doom that he has believed to be possible. Let me give you one case which will show you how vivid it may be—not the case of believing in hell, but a very practical case of a woman who was burnt to death in the cabin of a ship. You can imagine what such a person would endure in the moments before death, as it was coming upon her, before she knew she could not escape, a horror, a terror. With the flames gathering around her in that lonely cabin, fighting as she did for life—as could be seen by her body when it was discovered too late to save—she went out of the body in a passion of terror, an agony of fear. Two of us found her on the other side surrounded by flames that her own imagination had created, suffering under that imagination, and still in the terror of the death. So profound was that terror, so frantic her agony, that it was hours and hours before it was possible to comfort her and to persuade her to look round and see that there was nothing around her which could injure or terrify. I mention that particular case in order to make you see, as it were, for a moment the harm that may be done by lurid descriptions of terrors of what may happen on the other side of death. People who go out of the world with those in their mind do for a time suffer the very terrors that they fear, not for long, happily, for there are many on the other side whose work it is continually to help those who have passed on, to make them know that there is no fear, no terror, which need thus torture them when the body has been left behind. But I would urge upon everyone who uses the power of the tongue to teach religion not to use those terrors against the sinner, for they are creating the hell that for a brief while may torture, until the baseless imagination has been shown to be the nullity that it is. So much trouble is caused there, so much unnecessary suffering, that you cannot wonder if some of us who have to undo the mischief on the other side, try as far as we can to argue against it here.

Those who go into the other world by sudden death—by suicide, by accident—are the people who need most on the other side the care of those who help, and the great intelligences, whom you speak of as angels, have, as part of their work, the helping and the comforting of those who, flung suddenly out of the one life into another, find themselves as strangers on the other side of death. It is because of the shock of such a sudden departure that you find in the Litany of the Church of England the prayer to be saved from sudden death. I have often heard people nowadays say that they cannot use that prayer with any reality of feeling, that they think it would be better to pass out suddenly and have no warning of the approach of the death hour. Not so is the opinion of all those who know the conditions on the other side. Far better the illness, in which the clinging to life is gradually loosened, than the sudden shock of the flinging of the intelligence out of the body into that other world with all the suddenness which stuns and bewilders, and the marvel that sometimes terrifies the unprepared new-comer to that world. Sudden death is a thing not desirable from the standpoint of all who know, and that old Christian prayer is based on occult knowledge.

I have often been asked what is the fate of the suicide. There is no one answer you can give to that, because the fate depends on the life that has gone before, and not simply on the sudden act that has closed that life on earth. Where a man who has wronged others tries by suicide to escape from the results of the wrong that he has done, kills himself to, say, escape prosecution for embezzlement or anything of that sort, his life on the other side is certainly unhappy, but rather for the wrong that preceded than for the act that slew the body. Where a man has caused much misery, wretchedness, by any form of human fraud or trickery, and then strikes away the body because he cannot face the results of what he has done, he escapes nothing. Helpless on the other side, he sees the misery that he has wrought. Unable to assist, tormented by the sight of the harm he has done, he has only injured himself by the hasty striking away of the body. He finds himself face to face with all the pain he has caused, with the sin and the misery of the victims he may have reduced to poverty, and who surround him by angry thoughts. It is the most foolish of actions to strike away the body, for he thereby only renders himself more helpless. Nothing is escaped thereby. There is only greater intensification of the sorrow. But in the case of a suicide, who by bitter suffering or despair has practically lost control over his mind, who acts not with thought, but thoughtlessly, whirled away perhaps by a wave of despair that he is unable to breast, there the result of the action is naturally not so terrible, for it is suffering and not crime which has led up to the rash act of suicide. But in every case where the body is struck away, be it by self-inflicted death or accident, the man is not dead in the ordinary sense of the term—I mean as he would be if he had lived out his cycle of years upon earth. He has to live that out on the other side. Only, the conditions are less favourable there than here. It is the life on earth without a physical body, tied, as it were, to earth, and unable to leave it until the hour comes for which the body was builded, the natural time of death. Hence in all cases suicide is an act of folly, the putting oneself at a greater disadvantage rather than the getting away from difficulty and suffering, and the only cases in which there is merely a peaceful sleep upon the other side in the case of suicide is where the mind has really been unhinged by pain, and no moral responsibility can attach itself to the rash act that ends the life.

The experiences on the other side, again, bear directly on the infliction of capital punishment here. No greater folly, as well as crime, than to send the criminal out of this world into the next by the act of law. It is not only that you throw away the chance of helping, the chance of training, the chance of reforming, but you do the maddest of all mad things—you set free a malignant intelligence that here you could keep from doing harm to his fellows. Your criminal who has committed a murder is helpless while you hold him under restraint, but if you strike away the body, how can you control him on the other side? It is men of that sort who have given rise to the ideas of devils tempting and urging others to sin. Those men, furious at the act that has ended their lives, hating society, and longing for revenge, they it is who only too often push weaker criminals into similar crimes. Often the bad harvest of the gallows is a number of similar crimes taking place in the community that sends the murderer to his doom. It is not without significance that the countries that have abolished the death penalty are those where murder takes place the least often. Switzerland is such a country, but murder is the rarest of crimes there. Where you hang for murder, you practically make temptation and instigation to murder round the place where the murderer's body was struck off. Hence, from the study of other-world conditions we learn a lesson for the improvement of our treatment of criminals here.

But pass from that worst side of human life, and take the average human being, man or woman—not a high type for a moment, a low but not a sinful type, the type that you get by hundreds and thousands among yourselves—the men whose only pleasures outside the work by which they win a livelihood are the pleasures of the racecourse, the pleasures of the music hall, the pleasures which can only be enjoyed in the body, and which do nothing to stimulate the mind nor to gratify the loftier emotions, those whose amusements are trivial, childish, depending for their interest on the mere changing of money. Or take the women whose lives are as trivial as those of the men, who find their greatest pleasure in fashion or idling. What can you do with those people on the other side of death, when you come to think how much of them is left? All their life has gone into their bodies. All their interests have to do with physical things. They have no intellectual pleasures, no artistic pleasures, nor pleasures of the higher emotions. Clothes, fashion, games, these are the things alone in which they take a lively interest, and these things do not go on to the other side of death. Now, those people do not suffer in the sense of any keenness of suffering. It is a dull, grey, unhappy life for the time, until the higher side of them awakens and begins to show activity in that other world. To put it colloquially, they are very much bored. There is no word that expresses their condition better. You meet them wandering about discontented, grumbling, fretful, complaining—not actually suffering, as I said before, but finding life so grey as to be almost intolerable. Now, there is a certain value in knowing that beforehand. It is no good knowing it only when you get there. If you know it beforehand you can provide against it, and the provision against it is simple enough. Measure your amusements as well as your work, and let some of them at least be of a nature that death is unable to destroy. I am not speaking against the taking of pleasure. All human beings need some pleasure and some amusement, and most of all those whose work is laborious and of the nature of drudgery. They do need pleasure in order to brighten their lives here. But is it necessary that the pleasure should be of such an unspeakably stupid character? That is the point that you want to think about. Take music. Music is a thing which stirs emotions that you can carry on to the other side of death, that you may utilise there in many of the forms of noblest pleasure. Then why not here have the music that raises a little, rather than the music that degrades? It need not be of too difficult a kind; it need not be what would be called classical, music interesting only to the musician; it may be a noble ballad; it may be a song carrying with it some high sentiment or pure emotion, something better than the miserable patter which is what you may hear in many of the music hall songs, drivel which is not fit for rational people to listen to at all. Now that is one of the practical points that come out of the study of the other-world conditions. Make part of your amusements at least from that portion of your nature which you carry on to the other side. Have some taste, some hobby, if you will, which you find interesting, something that cultivates and refines, without being too much of a strain upon the brain that may be already tired with the day's toil, but something which appeals to the real human part of you, and not only to the mere physical part. And that will be something to carry on to the other side, and to make you on that other side contented and happy by the resources that you have within yourself.

You find many of those who have passed onwards who are still in the higher regions of the intermediate world with which I have been dealing, many a man whose interests are large, those who love their community, who love their town, or love their country. These men carry on into the intermediate world subjects of interest and powers of usefulness as well. A statesman, or the politician who has been honourable and serviceable, the man who has loved the people and tried to serve them, his utility is not ended when death strikes away the body. In that higher world he can still work for the causes that he loved, still inspire others with the enthusiasm that moved him here. He carries on his interests and his powers, and is able to work for others on the other side of death.

So in making up your life here have some larger interests, some care for the common good, some thought for the common welfare, some larger self than the self that is limited by the body, and then, as you pass onwards, life will grow wider not narrower, richer not poorer, fuller of happy activity instead of being deprived of it, for you build here your life on the other side and carry with you the materials for it.

Let us leave the intermediate world and pass on into the heavenly, that heavenly world which is the world of growth, which is the world of swifter evolution. And all men pass on into that heavenly world, even the poorest in virtue, the lowest in intelligence. That lowest class of which I spoke at first, who inevitably pass through the experience of suffering, grow out of it and pass on into the heavenly world, for only a short stay, I grant, for the material they take with them is small. Never a seed of good, either in emotion or in thought, that is lost to the soul that experienced it, that does not find its flowering place on the other side of death. Now, in that heavenly world we also find lives differing according to the lives which here were led—all happy, but happy in different measures, according to the greatness of the capacity for happiness. None but is as happy as he can be, through all the days of his heaven-life, his capacity to receive always full, but the amount of the capacity varying from one to another. And first you find in the heaven-world a perfect satisfaction for all the loves and the affections of the world you are in to-day. Never a tie of love that is broken by death, never a tie of affection that does not find in the heaven-world its realisation. Love on earth is sometimes frustrated, but in heaven it finds the crown which here it failed to win. People ask sometimes: "Shall we know each other in heaven? Shall we there meet our dear ones?" What would heaven be unless the loved ones of earth found there their reuniting, or if one who was beloved here was left outside? The circle of love must be complete, and so we find it is. None are missing whom here we loved, none are away from us whom here we cherished. If you think for a moment, you will see how reasonable that is. For you do not love only the bodies; you love the immortal spirits of those who are dear to you. A mother loves her son. But he changes from the babe that she nursed in her arms to the man who in her old age is her support and consolation. The babe and the man are very different in body, but always the son is there, and it is the son, and not the body, that the mother loves, though the body may be dear for the son's sake; and her son is ever with her in that heavenly world. So again with all others, with every tie that here on earth might seem to be broken. Have you a friend from whom misunderstanding has parted you? Have you a friend who has turned against you, though once he loved you? Have you some friend who has forgotten you, or, worse than that, has returned your love with coldness and your helpfulness with ingratitude? Never mind. Keep on loving, though he has ceased to love. Pour out love unstintingly, though he has turned his back upon you. For in the heavenly world you will re-win the friend whom here you seemed to lose. Keep the love tie unbroken, and it will knit you each to each again in the heavenly world.

All, then, of our higher emotions find in heaven their intensification and their bliss. But not love only which unites heart to heart, as friend or relative; the love of mankind, that nobler, grander love which spreads itself out in service and endeavours to lift and help the race, that great love of man, often frustrated here on earth for lack of power and lack of opportunity, that love comes back to you in heaven and grows into the power of service that in this life you lacked. That is the wonderful alchemy of heaven. Every hope and every affection, every thought and every aspiration, these are the materials of the heaven-world out of which you build your nature and gradually evolve it towards perfection.

I have said to you elsewhere that thought creates, but the creative power of thought is at its highest and its greatest in the heavenly world. Not one noble aspiration, not one pure and lofty thought, not one passing flash of longing to help and serve, but in the heaven-world you shall find it again, to weave it into the garment of the spirit with which you shall be reborn again to serve on earth. Heaven is the growing place for all the seeds which here we are planting. The harvest of the heaven-world depends on the richness and the nature of the seeds which here you sow, and if you would have your heaven full and rich, if there you would evolve more rapidly than here, then think nobly and highly, love purely and largely, and all that experience here upon earth shall turn into power and faculty in heaven.

This is the bearing of the knowledge of the life after death on life here. It is no idle folly, no useless pleasant imagining. You work out here that which in the other worlds you shall enjoy and utilise. When you understand that, or begin to understand it, you change your life here and make it more a preparation for a long life of heaven, for, remember that life here is but like the dip of the diving bird into the sea, out of the free air of heaven down into the ocean. It dives for a moment to catch the food it requires. So each of you, heaven-born, not earth-born, plunge from the heavenly life down into the earthly to carry back the experience you gather to your heavenly home. That is the use of the earthly life, to give the experience that in heaven you will build into character and power, to gather the seeds of the harvest that there you will reap, to make possible here the richness and the glory of a long heavenly life. When you know it, you would not let a day go by that does not sow some seed for the heavenly reaping. A little reading of great books, a little coming into touch with the great minds of the race, the communing with those who have left behind them the mighty literature of the past, these are the affinities that in the heavenly world realise themselves. Here you may have small chance of going among the greatest and the most thoughtful of your race. Never mind, you can pick here the company that in the heavenly world you will enjoy, and if you study here the writings of a Plato, the writings of any great thinker of the past, the writings of the great authors of our own time—Emerson, Ruskin, take whom you will—these studies of yours make links, which in the heaven world will re-assert themselves, and you shall know as teachers there the souls whose writings you have studied as loving pupils here. That is the way in which heaven and earth are linked together, that the vision in which the knowledge of the future enables us to make that future what here we determine that it shall be. Creators of your own destiny, you can make it as you will. On that side you cannot begin. You must begin here what there you shall continue. As these facts gradually become real to us, as by reiterated investigation and constant study we find out more and more that these worlds are all linked together, parts of a single life, continued, unbroken, life here becomes irradiated with the light of that fuller life, and earth becomes more beautifully illumined by the light of heaven. You are really in your higher spiritual nature living in heaven all the time, only earth's noises deafen you to the subtler music of the heavenly worlds. It is round you always. Heaven's inhabitants mingle with your grosser earthly life, heaven's music breathes around you, heaven's light shines about you, you who are natives and citizens of heaven, deaf and blind to your own country, and to the messages it is breathing to your souls. Your lives might be so much fuller, so much richer, so much happier, if only you would open the higher senses and not cling so passionately to the grosser forms of earth, but realise those belonging to your birth-place, which is really your true home.

An old teacher once said, when he was asked by his heavenly comrades, what he thought of earth: "A happy land for those who can forget their birth-place;" but there is a happier land for those who remember their birth-place; a stronger, higher happiness for those who realise more lives than one. All the prophets who have known heaven and talked on earth, all the Divine revealers who have lifted a little corner of the veil and taught their followers the realities of the greater life, bear witness to the reality of the life on the other side of death, to its being a continuance of the life that here we are leading. If you study your lives here, mark your faculties, judge your amusements and your business here, you can forecast what your life shall be upon the other side. Make it what it should be, full of the power of evolution, full of the certainty of growth, full of the splendour of the divine potentialities within you. Then earth shall also become heaven, and the two shall mingle in your lives, and those around you who know not of that glory, those around you who still are blinded by the earth, shall catch from the beauty of your lives something of the promise of the life immortal, and you shall bring to the deafened ears of earth some of those melodies of heaven which shall have become the music of your own lives.

The Power of Thought

We very often hear the phrase in common conversation that So-and-so is "a self-made man." But when we come to ask what is meant by the speaker in calling anyone a self-made man, we always find that the speaker is dealing with the value of the money the man has made and not at all with the making of himself. His banker's balance is the thing that is considered, and not the character and nature of the man. I propose this evening to talk to you about the way in which any man can really make himself; not make money, not make social position, but really make what we call a man, his thought power, his character, his moral nature, his future. All this is within his power, if he knows how rightly to utilise his thought. It is that with which I want to deal, and I shall try to show you that, both from the later scientific standpoint and also from the testimony of religions, thought is the great creative power, and that to understand how to use it, to utilise it to the full, is really to make ourselves the masters of our future, to shape and build ourselves into whatever form we will. Many of you may know that one religion after another has practically said exactly the same thing about the power of thought. One of the most ancient of the Indian Scriptures declares: "Man is created by thought; what a man thinks upon that he becomes." And then, the sentence finishes in the characteristically Indian way: "Therefore think upon God." So you may find in the Hebrew Scriptures: "As a man thinks, so he is." That testimony of religion is amply borne out by the discoveries of science; and I propose to deal with those first, so as to make what many would regard as a solid basis for certain things that I want to put to you as a matter of practice and conduct.

I will ask you first to look in the widest and roughest way possible on one clear power that thought has, even over the dense matter of which our outer physical body is made up. If you look at two old people, one of whom through life has been harsh and selfish, and another who through life has been generous and benevolent, you will at once be able to tell by what we call "expression" that which has been the character of the life. Now expression is only the result of the movements of certain muscles, of the habits impressed by thought on the features and on the movements of the features. Any of you who have read Darwin's famous book on "The Expression of the Emotions" will remember how he analyses emotions with their corresponding expressions, and shows how, by the continual repetition of any emotion, a corresponding sculpturing of the contour of the features will take place. And you may notice in the most ordinary life that if a man or woman is habitually harsh, then even in gentle moments the physical apparatus does not lose the habit impressed upon it by the ordinary emotion which dominates the character. So much, even in the coarse and gross matter, do we find that thoughts and emotions have the power to shape and to mould. But far more important than that is the question of the relation of thought to the thinking apparatus, to the brain itself. Now during the latter part of the earlier half of the 19th century, some very remarkable statements were made as to the relation between brain and thought. Some of you will remember a statement of Carl Vogt, that I suppose not a single psychologist now would repeat, that "the brain produces thought, as the liver produces bile." It was a rough and brutal way of putting the thing, but still to a very large extent scientific thought in the seventies and eighties still ran along that line, though only in a few cases quite to that extent. And the whole question as to the relation of thought and brain, thought and nervous system, is really part of the larger argument, whether the organ produces the function, or the function produces the organ. Now along the line of the materialistic argument which science then was so thoroughly following, you will find it put forward in the writings of the times that it is the organ that produces the function. My old friend, Büchner, in dealing with that very thing, remarked that we did not have legs because we wanted to walk, but we walked because we had legs; and that puts in a brief phrase the whole gist of the argument that then practically held the scientific world. But as a true matter of evolutionary fact that is not so. We find when we look back into a very early stage of the living creature, that the whole living creature is nothing but one cell, homogeneous in its contents, rounded in its form. We find that that single scrap of living matter shows out the functions of life, though the organs of those functions are entirely absent. When the creature at that early stage of evolution wants to eat, he has no mouth, but wherever the food is, there he takes it in. And as we trace him and those who come after him along the line of evolution, we find that the constant exercise of the function of eating gradually builds up a mouth by which that function can be better performed. And so, all through the functions of life in that tiny scrap of living matter. If we take the example that Büchner took, the question of locomotion, what is it that we find? This scrap of living matter has no legs; he wants to move, and so he pushes out just a little bit of the substance of his body, and then drags his body after it in a very clumsy way, until in the movement of the body the leg again disappears into the substance, and he has accomplished a very primitive form of movement. Now it is by continued repetition of that act, by wanting to move over and over again, that at last a definite leg is established, and the organ of locomotion is thus seen to be created by the will, the desire, to move. And so throughout evolution there is always first the want, then the effort, the exercise of power, and by that exercise there follows the creation of the instrument whereby the power is more perfectly expressed. And if we carry that process through all evolution until we come to the nervous system and the brain, is there any reason why the brain alone of all the organs of the body should escape from the otherwise universal rule that it is function that creates organ and not organ function? Shall we not be more in accord with the analogy of nature, shall we not be following more exactly the method of nature's working, if instead of saying that thought is produced by the brain, we allege that the brain is produced by the exercise of the function of thought? If you study nature you will be compelled to come to that conclusion, that the organ of thinking is the product of the exercise of thinking; that is, that as we think we create, even as regards the matter of the brain. I need not even stop there, for later science has given us further particulars of the power of thought upon the brain. If you read some of the later investigations into the brain, you will learn that when the child is born into the world there are certain large cells in the brain that do not divide, that do not grow more numerous, that remain in the brain at the number which exists at birth. Then it is found that as the thought life of the child begins, changes occur in these cells. They do not divide and multiply, as I have just said, according to the ordinary rule of cell-multiplication under the impetus of exercise, but none the less they change. At first they were merely irregular rounds, but, as the child begins to think, little processes begin to shoot out of these cells, little roots they look like, and so they are called by the Greek name *dendra*. As the thoughts go on, these rootlets become more and more numerous. As the thoughts go on, the rootlets of one cell join with those of another, until as the thought process continually expands, these little cells are joined together by a network of these tiny rootlets, and you have a web of nervous matter joining all the cells together and making them the great organ of the reasoning faculties. And so much is this the case, that you find doctors and scientific men now advising parents and teachers not to try to force their boys and girls into logical processes of reasoning until they have reached a certain age. They point out that the observations of the child, the baby efforts at the connecting of observations together, the childish efforts to draw conclusions from the observations made, that those are the things that lead to the organisation of the cells, and that gradually build the physical organ of thought. And if, with a child too young, in whose brain as yet thought has not produced this necessary web for thinking, if you try to press that child, teaching him logic, mathematic, or other lines of thought which depend for their understanding on the exercise of the reasoning faculty, you will find the child cannot do it. In that case he will only learn by rote; he will not understand the logical process. And it is very likely that many of you, if you look back to your school days as boys and girls, may remember how you committed the problems of Euclid to memory instead of trying to reason them out as a trained mathematician would do; and you may remember that sometimes when your teacher tried to see if you had understood, and altered the letters at the various angles of the figures, you showed yourself to be a most unfortunate failure, and were entirely unable to reason it out. You could only remember, you could not reason. Now, according to the physiologist and the scientist, you cannot go through the process of reasoning until you have created your reasoning instrument. Supposing, in order to see whether it is the brain or the man who is at fault, you take a fairly stupid peasant and throw him into the hypnotic trance, and then try whether he can reason or not. Over and over again it has been shown that when the brain is paralysed, under those conditions the reasoning faculty is able to show itself out apart from the brain, is able to transmit it through the instrument which cannot itself answer to the thought. And many of the conclusions that have been built up by modern psychologists on the functions of the brain, and the relations to it of the reasoning faculty, are largely based on the results which have been attained when the brain has been paralysed, and the power of the thought has been tested apart from the mechanism of the brain.

So for the moment I will leave that part of the subject at this, that your thought is the creative power for the improving of your brain. If you want your brain to become a better instrument of thought, you must deliberately use your power of thought in order to exercise it, and thereby to improve it. As you think, you not only affect these particular cells that I spoke of, but in other parts of the brain you multiply cells in the ordinary way by exercise. You find if you compare the brain of the thinker and the brain of the peasant that they are entirely unlike in the number of their convolutions, in the depth and the complexity of those parts of the surface of the brain. You can look into this as you please in books of anatomy and in books of physiology; from all of them you will come to the same result, that by exercise of the function of thought you improve the physical instrument that you use in the thinking. Now it is that fact which has so much bearing on the possibilities of human beings in regard to higher kinds of thinking. There is not one amongst you—although this applies more effectively to the younger than it does to the older—there is not one amongst you who cannot make your brain a better instrument than it is now, by habitual and regular thinking. It is not such a difficult thing after all to give, say, ten minutes' thought to the reading of some book which a little bit strains your attention, which a little bit taxes your power of thought; not one of you, even on the way to your office, instead of giving the whole of your time to the daily paper, but might read if it were but a paragraph or two of some book full of noble thinking, full of strenuous thought; and the effect of that on you would be that gradually your brain would be builded for finer purposes of thought. You would find that slowly, unconsciously, but steadily and without fail, because law is law and nature never deceives those who work in harmony with herself, you would find that your thought power was increasing; you would find your brain keener, more alert, more competent, for the ordinary business of life. You would find it susceptible to longer continued exercise, and you would build your brain as regularly as the athlete builds his body, and find that you were ever becoming more athletic in your thought power, with an instrument which did not fail you when you appealed to it to serve. And that is true all round, not only with regard to your brain, but also with regard to your muscles. Sandow, the strong man, tells those who practice the exercises that he has devised for the strengthening of the muscles, to think about the muscle that they are trying to develop, not to carry on the exercises thoughtlessly, but to turn their thought and fix it on the thing that they are trying to achieve. He is quite right. If you bring your thought power to bear on the muscle you are trying to develop, life will flow into it more fully, growth will take place in it more rapidly. This thought power of yours is really creative, even as regards the muscular part of the body. By this thinking power you can literally build up your muscular strength by directing your thought to the muscular effort you are making.

Let us turn aside from that part of our subject, from the building of the brain, or the building of muscle. Let us take the power of thought in a rather less usual form. Now one great difficulty with regard to the application of the power of thought is the many thoughts that present themselves when you are trying to think of a single object. All of you know that, if you have ever tried to think. Well, you cannot concentrate your thought if you do not practise it. At first, when you are endeavouring to fix your thought on one matter, so many other thoughts come in that the power of the one thought you are dealing with is weakened, just as, when there is a current of water and a number of other currents come suddenly flowing in, there will be a tossing about of the water and foam and rippling in different directions instead of a single well-directed stream. But there is one way in which we can test the power of thought, when we have quite checked all other thoughts; and that, in the easiest possible way, is in what is called the mesmeric or hypnotic trance. Now, when a person is mesmerised or hypnotised, the result of that is to throw the brain out of working order. You may carry the hypnotic force to the point where the heart has ceased to beat so far as you can feel it, where the breath has ceased to pass in and out of the lungs so far as you can test it, even by a mirror put to the lips; the mirror will remain undimmed. Only by a delicate instrument applied to the heart or lungs can you find out that there are still slight movements going on; that the heart has not entirely stopped; the lungs have not quite ceased to expand and contract. When you have reduced the body to that condition it means that the blood is circulating scarcely at all in the blood vessels. It means that it has not become properly aerated, and oxygen is not in it to the extent necessary for healthy functioning. You have thrown your brain into a condition which would be called coma, if it were brought about by disease. You have checked, as I have said, the circulation of the blood, you have not supplied blood enough, and good blood enough, to make it possible for the brain to function, for thought to work properly. Now when you have done that, and when you have, by flashing an electric light into the eye, found that there is no sensitiveness there, when you have fired a pistol beside the ear, and have thus shown that the ear is deaf to outer sound, what do you find when you come to examine into the changes of consciousness, normally carried on through the brain? You find that so far from these being in any way hindered by the paralysis of their instrument, they are very much keener and more active and more powerful than they were before. But you have opened up your way to a particular line of experiment. You have made the brain insensitive to all ordinary things. There are no thoughts going on in it; none of the ordinary functions are in activity. The effect of shutting all those out is that if you impress on the brain something from outside, a suggestion as it is called, you can bring about the most extraordinary results. That suggestion, striking on the brain rendered thus insensitive, will produce, left alone to work fully, the most startling effects on the body. You can produce a wound, a burn, a lesion of any kind that you like. Not very long ago in Paris a stupid medical student, not understanding, presumedly, what he was doing, said to a woman who had been hpynotised, and who had been sufficiently awakened to hear—for that may be done, whilst still the rest of the nervous system is gripped in the hypnotic trance—"This iron I hold up (one of the surgical instruments) is red hot." He put it on her chest. He produced a frightful burn; and over and over again experiments of that sort have been tried—cruel and wicked, but proving the fact that by the mere suggestion of an injury that injury appears. And if any time, when you happen to be travelling to Paris, you care to go to the Salpêtrière Hospital, the doctors there will show you many photographs that they have taken, photographs of injuries inflicted on the body purely by the power of thought. You can make a blister by taking up a bit of blotting paper, dipping it in water, placing it on the flesh and saying: "It is a blister." You can thus induce inflammation, the red skin, the water within the blister, and the pain of the ordinary blister, all produced by thought, by suggestion, without the ordinary physical medium. Or you may do the reverse if you like. You may take a real blister and put it on the patient's body and say: "It is only a piece of paper dipped in water," and the effects of the blister do not follow; the skin remains uninjured, and no blister is produced. You can play with the human body by thought, either harming or not harming it exactly as you please.

These are not questions where dispute is possible among the educated. These things have been done over and over again, and over and over again are the same effects produced. But take experiments of a different kind which are not cruel in that way. Take one that I myself saw performed, copying a thing that I had read in a French book. There was a young man who was very sensitive to hypnotic influence—mesmeric influence, rather. He was mesmerised, thrown for a moment into a trance. In the trance he was told: " When you wake up you will not be able to see Mrs. Besant; you will see everybody else, but she will be invisible." He was waked up out of the trance, and he seemed quite normal. He talked in the ordinary way, behaved as he had behaved before he was in the trance, but he could not see me. He was told by one of the other people present to count the people in the room, and he pointed to them; he pointed to everybody else but missed me. Then I took up a handkerchief and I walked about the room carrying the handkerchief, and he followed me with his eyes. Somebody said to him: " Well, what are you looking at?" He said: " That is very queer; that handkerchief is moving about in the air; what joke are you playing upon me? I can see it moving about, but there is nothing supporting it." I went further. I took a playing card, and I put the playing card—without looking at it, and without allowing anyone else to look at it, to avoid what is called thought transference—behind my back; and he was asked to read it. He said: "There is a card flying in the air." They said: " Tell us what the card is." He answered at once, giving the suit of the card, and the number of the pips upon it, showing that I was so invisible to him that he was even able to read through my body. Many other experiments of the same kind I have myself tried, over and over again, in order to test the written records and see whether these records are accurate and true. And so I have learned by my own experimenting that it is perfectly possible to inhibit the senses, exactly as far as you choose, by your own suggestion imposed on the mesmerised subject. You can make him either see or not see, hear or not hear, feel or not feel. One day, in the very early days of my experiments, when I did not understand the thing perhaps as well as I do now, I very nearly had an accident in that way, for I had mesmerised a young man who was very sensitive to mesmerism. A young fellow he was, very athletic, not of very strong intelligence, and I told him he should not be able to see me; and, thoughtlessly rather—I did not consider the result—I put out my hand and touched his shoulder and spoke to him. He heard my voice, and he felt my touch, but he could not see me, and the effect was that he very nearly had a fit of terror, and I had to remove the impression at once, so that he could see as well as hear and feel. I only mention these cases to show you how utterly the human body and the human senses are mere playthings for thought, and how with any person under control in that fashion you can deal with him as you like. "Well," you say, "it is simply that these people were mesmerised." That is true, and the value of the mesmerism is that it shuts out the ordinary thought impressions. If you are able to think strongly and clearly, then you can impress your thought, without any need of the mesmeric trance to help you, on the person upon whom you choose to impress it. The only advantage of the mesmeric trance is the shutting out of all the thoughts of the person mesmerised, and all thoughts coming from outside, except your own thought alone, which you impress upon his brain.

Now take another case, which goes very much further than the ordinary experiment. You have probably heard of some of the Indian tricks played by Indian jugglers, and raising much surprise; and you may have sometimes heard it said by conjurers here: "Oh, we can do the same thing." They can do it by apparatus; the Indian does it without, and that is all the difference. I grant to the full that people like Maskelyne and Cook, in their own hall, with their own platform, and their own apparatus, can reproduce, to some extent at least, to an audience sitting away from the platform on which their tricks are being played, some of the tricks played by the Indian jugglers. But the conditions are very different. An Indian comes into your house, naked, except for a cloth thrown around his middle, so that he can hide nothing in the bare arms and bare chest; he comes along with a basket on his back, a common basket, and throws it down, and lets you pick it up and look at it exactly as you please. He puts it down on your own verandah, or in your own house, and he invites you all to sit around it, with him and the basket, and the child who is with him, and you make a circle round him, and you look at him. Then he does his basket trick. You see him put the little child in the common basket, and rope it up, and then you see him stick his sword through the basket, and you hear screams, and you see blood come out. But presently the little child comes running in from the other side of the verandah. You open the basket and it is empty. What has happened? A hypnotic trick and nothing more. He won't do it twice over running. He says: "No, I will do it to-morrow, I won't do it again to-day."

If you would know the way it is done, it is nothing more than a mere illusion imposed upon the senses. You can watch exactly what he does, and you will notice before he begins, as he sits there with all of you sitting around him, he begins chanting a curious little chant, very, very monotonous, the same rhythm repeated over and over again; and though you may not be conscious of it, that monotonous vibration is paralysing your brain and your senses. He is doing exactly what the hypnotist does when he paralyses the brain of his patient, and he is producing what is called a collective hallucination, not on one patient, but on all the people around him, by the trick that he has learned to perform. What you think you see is what he is thinking about; that which he determines you shall see. It is obvious it does not take place, but you see it taking place by the force of his thought imposing an hallucination upon you, and in that way they do their tricks. The famous rope trick is done in the open street. You can see the rope go up, and stand suspended in the air, and a boy run up it and disappear at the top; and then a man goes up after him with a knife, and he also disappears, and sometimes the mutilated limbs of the boy are thrown down on the ground; then afterwards they both walk in quite comfortably, from behind the crowd, take up the rope and go off. That was seen a year or two ago in a street in Surat, and when Maskelyne and Cook spoke about their trick as "the Indian rope trick," a lady doctor, a friend of mine, wrote to the papers and pointed out that she had seen that trick done in India, but that it was done not as Maskelyne and Cook did it, but was performed under her own window in the open street, with no apparatus at all, except the rope the man had twisted around him before he undid it, and threw it up in the air. It is all hypnotism and nothing else. If you photographed the trick, you would not see all this. You saw it because he chose that you should see it, and because the Indian conjurer had learned to impose his own thought on the brains of a number of people who were gathered around him. Now, I mention that to show how strong the power of thought may be in producing an illusion. And if it can produce and imprint an illusion upon wide-awake people, and make the picture that the man determines they shall see, does it not open some avenues of possibility for the strange wonders that may be wrought by thinking? And when you know that these things can be done, either that you can make people see what you like, and hear what you like, or that, if you be indifferent enough to human pain, you can form wounds and lesions of the body, by the mere power of thinking, does it then seem so strange that you can think along safer lines, and heal instead of injure, destroy sickness and create health, instead of produce an illusion of the senses? That is what underlies all the talk you hear about mental science, and Christian Science, and the rest. They are dealing with a real law, with a real power in nature, this power of thought; they are utilising that for the healing of disease; and disease may thus be healed, as all know, who have looked carefully into it. When you read sometimes of what are called miracles of healing, it is only the same thought-power applied to people sensitive and eager to meet the thought of the healer, with the longing to be healed. There is no real doubt that large numbers of these so-called miracles are wrought at Lourdes, and many other places. Now it is no answer to say that is is only imagination. Of course it is only imagination, but the imagination brings about the cure. And how have you shaken the fact of the cure when you say it is imagination? Nobody says it is anything else. If imagination is able to cure, and if cure is what you are seeking, what does it matter whether it is imagination or some drug which you find in your pharmacopœia? The doctor does not say if he succeeds in healing by medicine: "Oh, it is only the medicine that did it." He has got what he wants —the cure; and if you can get the cure by the power of thought applied to the patient what is the sense of saying it is only imagination, when your patient, who was sick, is cured, your diseased patient is healed? I grant it is no miracle. I grant that to call it a miracle shows ignorance, and not knowledge. I grant it is only a power of nature, a law of nature, understood and utilised. But it only shows ignorance to deny the possibility of it; and it shows more than ignorance, it shows prejudice, if you admit as valid, miracles that happened 1900 years ago, when you cannot examine into the evidence, and yet deny the similar miracles that happen to-day, when the evidence lies open for anyone to examine. That is where religious people are not quite fair. They admit their own miracles, provided they are old enough, but they will not admit any other people's miracles, especially when they are modern. But you know that is not reason; that is mere prejudice. It is not fair dealing. It is only using the prejudice of creed to deny what you do not like, because you think it would bring credit to a community which has not exactly the same label on it that your own may happen to have. There is too much of that, and that sort of prejudice will disappear when it is understood what laws of nature underlie all those so-called miracles, a higher force, brought down and applied on the physical plane; no more a miracle than your talking across the telephone wire, and that would seem a miracle to the savage. As for miracle in the sense of a thing contrary to the law of nature, there is no such thing; for every law is an expression of the Divine nature, which knows no change nor shadow of turning. If you say that it is the utilisation of a force that many people do not know, yes, it is; that it is the control by the will of natural powers that most people are still ignorant of, yes; that the person's own thought goes with it, and thereby renders the thought more effective, most certainly yes. I admit to the full what is called the power of faith. The person expects it. Then his thought works in with the other thought, and so applies it to his own particular case. Now it is sometimes asked: Is it possible to heal diseases which are not nervous? because, for some mysterious reason, quite unintelligible, people say: "Oh, yes, you may heal nervous diseases by thought, but not others." It is not very clear why you should heal one and not the other, and the method of operating is not explained by those who challenge the possibility of healing beyond diseases of the nerves. It is true that it is easier to apply it to the diseases of the nerves, because the nervous system is the normal mechanism whereby thought is expressed on the physical plane. You play upon your nerves by thought more readily than you do upon your muscles, or your bones; hence, it is easier to deal with the nerve than with the muscle or bone. Atrophy of the nerves is one of the diseases that no doctor can cure by drugs, but it is curable by what is called mesmerism, by utilising thought for the cure of the disease. In my own narrow experience of this—for I have not dealt with these questions of cure much in my life, because it is not one of the lines on which I work, I have no time—but in my own very narrow experience, I have known two cases of blindness, caused by the beginning of atrophy of the optic nerve, cured by thought, after they had unhesitatingly been declared incurable by the doctors to whom the patients had gone. Now diseases of the nerves are about the easiest things to cure where you utilise thought, because you are dealing with part of the mechanism of thought, and nerve answers more readily to thought than the structures and tissues which are not ordinarily worked on by thought in the same way. To heal a wound by thought is a far more difficult thing than to heal atrophy; but none the less it can be done, as may be shown by those experiments that I mentioned in the Salpêtrière Hospital in Paris. What is really wanted in those cases, where the mental scientist is going to try to heal absolute lesions in the body, is that he shall not only have power of thought, not only have a strong will, but also shall be trained anatomically and physiologically. So many of these people work blindly, where they ought to work with knowledge. If, instead of taking the power of thought only, they would be reasonable enough to study the anatomy and physiology of the human frame, they could apply their power of thought ten times more efficaciously than they do for the most part. They work blindly, where they might work with knowledge; work by using a law they have not sufficiently studied, rather than by using the least possible force necessary to bring about what they desire, supplementing the force by the knowledge of exactly what they want.

Now how should you proceed in such a case? Knowing the anatomy and the physiology of the part you want to affect, you produce by thought a picture of that injured part in a perfectly healthy condition. That is the first stage. By your thought you make the picture of what that part ought to be. Having thus created the picture, you proceed to imagine it into the place where the injury is, and by that means, bringing the thought to bear on the exact spot, you stimulate the recuperative powers in the body to perform swiftly what otherwise they would perform slowly, to build up quickly in the injured tissue what otherwise they would only build very gradually. And in all these cases, you must do it day after day, just because you cannot actually perform miracles, but only hasten the normal workings of nature. For instance, in those cases of atrophy I mentioned, it meant working steadily for a week in one case, and three or four weeks in the other, where the nerve was more depleted, the daily pouring in of the new life, the daily creation by the thought of the cure that you desired to effect; and under that the changes take place; under that the builders in the body work more energetically, more swiftly, and therefore more effectively. And there is not, I should be inclined to say, one human disease which might not thus be cured by thought wisely directed and brought to bear with knowledge on the part which has been injured. If, on the other hand, you ask me whether I think it is always worth while—well, no, I do not. But that is a different thing. I do not think it is always wise to use thought for the healing of physical disease and physical injury. I think that very often the result of such thinking is the making of the body far too sensitive to these things, through thinking far too much about the body.

Instead of utilising it as your servant, it becomes your master. That is the danger which runs along all these lines of Christian Science, applied only to disease, and Mental Science in the same way. Your body becomes the thing about which you think, and if you come across these people, they are always talking about bodies and always talking about pains and aches, and how they cured themselves, and that kind of thing—how they cured this, that and the other. The body then becomes a nuisance rather than a useful instrument, and I do not think it is worth while thus to utilise thought; for thought has far more noble uses than the mere curing of bodies, making cures that a strong will can effect, and a powerful mind can manage. That is why, although I acknowledge the possibility, I should not myself use thought to any great extent along those lines.

But now let us take another effect of thought, which it is worth while to think of for a moment, before I take up its greatest and most valuable power. I was speaking about the various lines of scientific thought which had led to this idea of its enormous power, and you may be aware probably that electrical and chemical changes are brought about by thought; and it is well to realise that, because it shows you the mechanism of the mind. People say sometimes: "How can thought affect matter?" If you realise these intervening links you will see how the effect takes place. If a galvanometer is put on your head and you think, an electric current will be set up in the brain, and its presence will be shown by the swing of the needle of the galvanometer. A doctor in London has carried on many investigations as to the effect of emotions on the normal perspiration or sweating of the body. He finds chemical changes are brought about by emotions. Acids, alkalies, etc., are set free under the influence of emotion. Another doctor, this time in Paris (Dr. Baraduc) has taken a large number of photographs, very interesting they are to look over, in which he says that he has photographed emotion and thought. Now, frankly, although he says he has done it, I do not think he has really done that. What I think he has done in his photographs is that he has caught the swirl of magnetic currents in the ether, which are produced by the thinking. Emotional thought, as far as I at present know, is too fine to be subjected to the photographic process. There is no doubt he has obtained results. He will show you a picture of a nun in prayer. You can see playing around her a great whirl of moving matter, tending upwards. Now, the doctor records that as the direct thought embodied in the prayer. My own view rather would be that it is a magnetic result, caused in physical ether by the vibrating matter, which is really answering to the change in consciousness, but which is not, I think, psychical matter. None the less, he has obtained a very interesting series of photographs of vibrations which you can correlate with changes in consciousness, but which are, I suggest, produced by physical forces working in the ether of the physical plane. That, however, brings me to the point towards which I was aiming, of the results which can be brought about by well-directed thought of the higher kind.

Now first for a moment let us pass to what religion calls prayer. Is that a force which can produce definite results? You may remember long ago that Professor Tyndall, when he was speaking about prayer and arguing against it, challenged the Christian world to an experiment. "Why not," he said, "take two wards in a hospital, filled by patients, who are suffering from a similar disease, who shall be treated just in the same way by doctors and by nurses; then, pray for those in the one and do not pray for those in the other, and compare the results." Well, I always have wished, since I knew the power of thought, that the Christian Churches had accepted Professor Tyndall's challenge. They would not do it. They said it was blasphemous. I do not see why. There is nothing blasphemous about it. If prayer can heal, why not have accepted the challenge? Personally, I should have been quite willing to accept the challenge in that way, because I believe you would find the people who were prayed for would be healed very much more quickly than the people who were not. Prayer is concentrated thought, with a power of love behind it. Now thought is dual in its nature: on one side a change of consciousness, on the other side a corresponding vibration in matter. There is no change of consciousness without a vibration in matter, however fine; there is no vibration in matter without a change of consciousness. If you have the change of consciousness that you call prayer, which is concentrated by the earnestness of the suppliant, you get a correspondingly powerful vibration in the matter of the finer, subtler worlds, and this can produce physical effects, just in the same way as the invisible wind, which is matter in a finer state than water, tosses up the denser water into waves or ripples. Finer forces can work on the grosser matter through the gradations downward from the matter which first they had set moving; and there is nothing unscientific nor unreasonable in the idea that by the thought force of prayer you can bring about physical results; but not always only by thought. There is another way also, which I can hardly quite leave out, by which these results are often brought about. Intelligence is not confined to you and me, taking you and me as representing the physical inhabitants of the world. There are plenty of other people who do not use bodies as gross as ours, who nevertheless are moving about us all the time; a prayer will very often be noticed by them, and they will bring about the result which is aimed at. But that is only another reason for praying, if there are people who by that prayer may be moved to do what you, unassisted, cannot do; and that is what Sir Oliver Lodge has pointed out. He has argued that there is nothing unscientific in the idea that prayer may be answered. He has pointed out that a child may ask his father to hand him down something he cannot reach. There is nothing unscientific in the father doing that, and giving him the object that the child asks for; there is nothing unscientific in asking the gardener to water the garden when you cannot water it yourself. Science was too much in a hurry in the days of Huxley; Science was too quick to lay down the law from conclusions insufficiently considered. The weakness in the science of the last century was that the area of knowledge was too limited, and it hastily built up a body of conclusions which wider knowledge has broken into pieces. For wider knowledge now shows that the claims of the religious world can be justified by facts, although the way in which the religious world has put them is certainly crude and unscientific. Still, if the claims are based on realities, the fact that they have put the reality badly is not such a serious matter after all if the effect is secured. Now, take a case like that of George Müller of Bristol. That man declared that he never used anything but prayer to get the money with which he kept up his orphan asylum. I have never heard his good faith challenged. He was a quiet, honest, pious man, unique in the strength of his thought and will, and that man tells us: "I had all these orphans dependent upon me, I asked for so much money, and it always came." I believe it did. I have done the same thing myself without praying. At one time, when I wanted a thousand pounds for a girls' club in the East End of London, I simply willed to get it. It came in all right. Honestly, I do not think it is quite the best way to get things. I do not say that I would do it now; I would not, because I believe that these higher intelligences, who work with men and for men, can judge better with regard to any particular thing whether it is well that money should be sent to it or not; and I prefer, therefore, to leave it to them either to help or not. I always find that the money does come in, without either willing or praying for it, for anything which is good in its object and serviceable to human beings. Being not quite so sure of my own wisdom as I was many years ago, I prefer leaving such matters to people who see very much further than I do, and I do not either will or pray for these particular things. But there is one use of prayer that ought never to be forgotten. It opens up the human heart to higher influences, and to greater forces. It puts the man in the receptive attitude which enables greater Intelligences to help, and the Divine life itself to enter into the human spirit, which has really only opened its shutters to the light. Just as when the sun is shining, if you open your shutters the sun will shine into your room, so if you open the closed shutters of your mind and heart Divine love and light and life flow in at the open window, and the spirit which opens itself to divinity is filled with divinity, not because divinity changes, but because the human vessel has been opened to receive the flood of light. Therefore, whether they understand it or not, it matters not, it is good for men to pray. As soon as they understand the working, they can adopt other methods if they will; but so long as man exists, and mightier Intelligences surround him for his helping, so long will the elder lead the younger, the greater help the lesser; and that mighty Father-heart, which has room for every grief and every suffering, will send the love of His heart into those who open themselves to receive it, and thus prayers will ever be used by those who know the higher experiences of the spiritual life.

Turn from that, and let us see what else thought may do. In a sense you can make your own character what you like by thought. I am not exaggerating it, and if you think I am, try. Remember that one hour of your own experience is worth more than many hours of my lecturing to you. You will be more sure when you have done one experiment in thought, than you would be by any amount of arguing which comes from me, which is, after all, only second-hand to you. So let me tell you exactly how to carry out such an experiment, and then you can try it if you will. Look at your own character, and judge its powers and its weaknesses. Pick out any weakness you like, it does not matter which. Say you are irritable—a very common thing in these hurrying days.

You say: "I am an irritable person." When you have once said that, never think of it again. Do not mourn over it, do not feel remorse; it will only make it worse, for you are throwing thought force into it every time you think of it, and that is why so many people never get rid of their faults. They are always mourning over their sins. If they threw them quite away behind them, and never thought of them, they would get rid of them very much more quickly, for thought vitalises anything we think about. If you think of your weakness, it becomes more and more a fact by your thought. Now do not think of your irritability. Think of patience, the exact opposite of the irritability; calmness, serenity, peace; and give a few minutes every morning to thinking steadily of that serenity; every day only for a few minutes at a time. Think of yourself as perfect in patience, perfect in serenity, perfect in calmness, and, if you will go on doing that steadily day after day, at the end of two or three weeks, or a month, you will find that you are beginning instinctively to be patient. You will find that irritability is diminishing, that you no longer feel inclined to be irritable. Slowly the patience will grow up in you, and you will become patient, almost unconsciously to yourself. Now, if there is any likelihood that that is true, it is worth trying, because, after all, it only needs a few minutes a day, say for a month; and if you find there is no result, then if you think well throw it aside. I have tried it for many, many years. For the last more than 19 years I have been trying experiments along that line, and I find it works. I find you can make whatever character you like by steady thinking of that kind. The only condition is it shall be steady and regular until the habit is established. You know you can make habits of ordinary life, that what you do with trouble at first, afterwards gradually becomes instinctive. Some of you have learnt to play the piano. It gave you a lot of trouble when you began; you had to watch your fingers. You know how a little child begins to play, looking at the fingers as hard as he can all the time, making faces over it in the funny way a child does, because the whole body is working for the one thing the child is trying to do. After a time the finished musician never needs to look at his fingers at all; he has made a habit of his work. The same with writing; you used to think how to form your letters when you were learning to write, now you do it as a matter of course, or your fingers do it for you, and it is only if you want to change your writing, if you find you are getting slovenly, that you need trouble about thinking of it at all. You can do just the same with your character. At first it will be toilsome, just as were the writing and the playing, needing a great deal of attention. But as you go on thinking and thinking, you will build the qualities, and they will become habits, and when you have established the habits, they make character, and then you have no trouble about it at all. Some people think that effort is the thing that deserves credit. They will say of a man who is truthful it is no credit to him to speak the truth; he does it by instinct. That is the highest credit you can have. It is the man who can do the right without effort, who really deserves praise, if praise should be given at all. Struggle means that you have yet to get the better of the difficulty; to do the thing without effort means that you have deliberately built it, and now you possess it, and no man is perfect until everything he does is done without effort, as part of his instinctive nature.

And this lecture will have failed of its object if there are not a few of you who will take up definite thinking, directed to a chosen end. You do not progress, because your thoughts are all over the place all the time, because to-day you are trying one thing, and to-morrow another, and on the next day you are at something else, and you wonder why you do not get on. Well if you want to succeed, it means steady persistent thought along one line. A mason who is going to build a house does not put a brick here one day, another there another day, somewhere else the next day, and then in somebody else's garden the following day, and across the road some other day. Why if he did it would be a long time before he got his house built. That is what you are doing with your character. To-day you are trying to be truthful, to-morrow patient, and the next day sympathetic, and so on, and you wonder why you never get any result at all, and you mean so well, too—you are trying to be "good." Give up the trying. Concentrate and practice in thought on one thing at a time, and thus build in the qualities, and then you will make progress and the goodness will be inevitable as progress is made. You want to be more practical, far more practical than for the most part you are to-day; to understand your power and know your creative ability. The whole World, the whole Universe, is only a thought of God, and you will grow into God's image and His powers will be reproduced in miniature in yourselves. You can build yourselves as He builds His worlds by that creative thought, the power of the imagination and the power of the will.

These are the divine powers in every one of you, though more developed in one than in the other. And as you progress in the power of thought and build yourselves by that power your character shall grow nobler, your lives more beautiful, your power to help stronger and stronger, until in time you shall awaken to know that you have built yourself into a world's helper, and that the power of thought in you has grown into the power to save.

The Guardians of Humanity.

There are some histories which are written entirely from the outside, and there are some students of history who only care to study the outer movements, the political constitution, the events and battles, the lives of kings and statesmen, of generals and admirals, which to them make up history. There are others who look a little deeper, and who see in history the succession of economic movements, of social conditions. Others who look yet more deeply consider that the thought currents of the nation, which work themselves out in economic or social or political conditions, are the real interest in historical study, and that the eyes of the real student should be fixed on the thoughts that create rather than upon the events that embody those thoughts. And there is one view of history which is still deeper than any of the three preceding ones, the view which is taken often by the poet and by the artist, and always by the student and believer in religion, that behind the kings and the statesmen, behind the economic movements and the currents of human thought there are mightier Intelligences, greater Powers, who use the outward agents and who guide the human destinies; Intelligences more developed than the human, Powers mightier than the powers of kings or statesmen, who work out a mighty plan of the world-process, and who use the thoughts and the powers of men as the tools whereby the world-process is carried on. And also, looking at the world for a moment more from the scientific than from the historical aspect, there are two contrasted views that attract minds of different temperaments. Some see in nature a vast mechanism; regarding all the forces of nature as mechanical forces, blind, unconscious, clashing the one against the other, and through the course of innumerable ages bringing out the order and harmony that we see. To such thinkers the various organisms that inhabit the globe have been built up by arrangements of matter producing the phenomena of life. They see in nature a soulless organisation; they see in man but the highest product of evolution; they do not see life as embodying itself in matter, but rather matter, by its arrangements, as producing, blossoming into, life. Over against that view is the view that looks upon nature as the outward expression of intelligence, the embodiment, the incarnation, of thought; which sees in all the forces of nature living intelligences continually at work; which sees at the head of all intelligences the wisdom that plans and the power that accomplishes. Sir William Crookes, summing up in his Presidential Address to the British Association for the Advancement of Science, the change which had come over the mind of Science during the many years which had elapsed since Professor Tyndall occupied the chair of the British Association until he himself was sitting in that same high place, marked the change of thought, these changing views of the scientific world, by quoting the statement of Tyndall that "we were learning to see in matter the promise and potency of every form of life," and declaring that now the tendency of thought was to see in life the moulder and shaper of matter. Now it is this second view that I am going to put before you this evening, tracing, if I can, for you to some extent the forces that lie behind the phenomena of human life, the plan on which the world process, the evolution of the world, is taking place.

In the view that I am going to submit to you we see life, intelligence, everywhere; we see the world as the field of evolution, not only of the human race, of the animal, the vegetable and the mineral kingdoms, but also as the field of evolution of invisible beings bound up in their evolution with the evolution of the human race, and of the kingdoms below humanity in nature; we see not only living intelligences evolving on our planet, but we see beyond these "planetary relations," as Myers calls them, the "cosmic relations" stretching beyond the limits of our own planet, and bringing us into relation with other worlds and with the inhabitants of other realms; and we see—taking part in human evolution and directing it, shaping the world for the inhabitants it bears, preparing our globe for the lines of evolution which are to develop upon it—mighty Workers, powerful Intelligences, working out a plan of marvellous wisdom, and utilising forces mighty in their scope, resistless in their power. And this great plan of the world-process, shaping the world and its products, and guiding the destinies of man, is, as it were, the ground plan, the outline, into which many details are to be worked, and in which a continual filling-out is taking place. We see, as it were, the great Architect of the Universe, confiding His plans into the hands of mighty viceroys; these handing it on again in sections to intelligences less mighty, though still superhuman; these, in their turn, handing on still smaller portions to rulers who rule over smaller areas, who deal with less mighty forces. Or, to take another analogy, we see a great drama being played out on the stage of the world, and the dramatist hands it over to the stage manager, and the stage manager casts the actors for their parts, which they make more or less vivid, more or less important, according to their individual capacities; free to initiate within certain limits; free to move within certain limitations. So in the universal law, there is a single Will to which all must bow, and the reproduction of that Will in the various individuals, human and superhuman, concerned; and there is the possibility, where you are dealing with the less evolved intelligences, of mistakes, mistakes due to limited thought and limited intelligence, even as among ourselves. And we see in this great Hierarchy of various grades of knowledge and of power, that while the higher ones, the rulers, may be vast in power and intelligence and mighty in the force of their will, yet the lower grades are more liable to error; the lower grades may often fail in their achievement, even as men, the servants in this world-family, also fail in intelligence and fail in power of achievement. And we see that just as the wiser may correct the mistakes of the less wise, and the stronger may help to shoulder the burdens of the weak, so in the higher ranks of these great Intelligences there are knowledge and power which, while leaving those who blunder to learn wisdom by the errors that they make, also use the results of those errors to restore equilibrium in relation to other errors that are made, and by balancing the one against the other bring out at last a perfect and satisfactory result. Such is the general idea. Glancing through the outer to the inner, from the seen to the unseen, but realising that everywhere intelligence and law are at work in the world-process, we see beings far greater than we are, but with intelligence like ours and knowledge that is limited, taking part in the evolution of humanity, sharing in the making of its destinies, and destined to share in the triumph of its perfection.

Now among the different religions different names are given to these intelligences. The Hebrews, the Christians, and the Mussulmans take the higher ranks of them all together and call them archangels or angels, and mass the lower ranks again together under various names—genii, fairies, and so on. And among the occultists of the Middle Ages we notice that they use still other terms, such as elementals, nature-spirits, and the like. In the older Eastern Religions, like the Hindu and the Buddhist, a somewhat deeper and closer analysis has been made of these many forces that mingle in the guidance of human destiny. They admit the presence of these superhuman intelligences, giving them the general name of "Shining Ones," a name which, for some curious reason, John Bunyan caught up in his "Pilgrim's Progress," using the very same term, "shining ones," which is the translation of the Hindu or Buddhist name of "Deva," often translated as God—a mis-translation, I may remind you. These higher beings with them are the equivalents of the Christian archangels and angels; but they say it is not only they who have to do with the guiding of human evolution. Human evolution has been going on through vast periods of time, and is not confined to a single planet, is not limited to one only of the globes that circle round our sun. Other inhabited worlds there are on which evolution is taking place, some on which evolution is much further advanced than it is upon our own globe. Here in our own world also evolution has been going on for ages and ages, and the fruitage of past evolution, the results of the process to which you and I are being subjected to-day, the unfolding of powers, the development of thought, all these in the past have also been going on, with the result that there are now in existence beings, human in their nature, the product of human evolution, though they have been longer in the evolutionary process than we, and are therefore further evolved, as we are evolved beyond the savage, as we are developed beyond the aboriginal, say, of this great continent on which you live; as the savage is to us, so are we to them; as the savage and we are evolving, so have they evolved beyond us. They are the Elder Brothers of the Race. They beyond all others may rightly be termed the Guardians of Humanity—men as we are men, products of a longer evolution, but products of evolution none the less as we also are products, the first-born, to use a Biblical expression, the first-born among many brethren, showing in the perfection of their humanity the promise of what all of us shall ultimately become. It is They who are the founders of the Great Religions of the world, They whose knowledge, overtopping the human, has reached the deepest recesses of the spiritual world, and brought out the treasures that therein They have found. They are the great revealers to humanity, the prophets and the seers of human kind; They are dwelling with us still in order to help forward our evolution and to guide our feeble steps to the heights which they have climbed. They are rightly called the Saviours of the world, They the Masters to whom the younger humanity looks up, They who are the promise of the future, and who show out in perfection what we can only show in the bud that precedes the perfect flower. It is the mighty Spiritual Intelligences that are called angels; and it is the highly evolved human beings whom we Theosophists call Masters—the name, let me remind you, claimed by Jesus Himself when He bade His disciples call none their Master upon earth, "for One is your Master even Christ."

Using these names, we have the two great classes of the Guardians of Humanity in the full sense of the term, and it is specially with their relations to the race that I want to deal to-night. Before passing into detail out of this more general sketch, let me remind you that within the large class of Devas, or angels, there are the great Beings who have to deal with the evolution of nature outside man and outside the animal and the other kingdoms of nature, who are concerned with the shaping of the world itself, with the changes brought about in the configuration of the globe, the forces that prepare the globe for man and change it in subordination to his needs and to enable it to co-operate in his evolution. Sometimes these forces show themselves in destruction of terrible kinds, sometimes in the slow building up of continents and the gradual changes in nature. But whether they work in storm and ruin, or whether they work in slow and gradual construction, they are none the less beneficent in their action, and guide it to definite ends. Use your imagination for a moment, throwing it back into the early ages of our globe ere yet it had assumed the outside appearances that now distinguish it, and see those mighty forces at work, forces that appear to be working destruction, that appear to be rending, crushing, driving, and yet are all co-operating to a foreseen end. Glance back in imagination to the ice-clad peaks, to the fields of eternal snow on the gigantic mountain ranges of past geological ages; see how from these comes sliding down a huge glacier, ploughing a vast furrow through the mountain, just like a plough with its mighty share, forcing its way onward until the broad, deep furrow is cut through the mountain belt. See how it destroys everything, pulverises rocks, crushes the craggy precipices into the mountain side; noise, tumult everywhere; apparently the forces of destruction are at work. And now close again the eyes of your imagination and open them some ages later, and where that mighty glacier ploughed out its destructive course a valley is laughing into flowers in the sunshine; fertile soil irrigated by the rippling river is putting on its golden vesture of ripe corn, and the white blossoms of the fruit trees everywhere in the spring-time mimic, as it were, the ice and the snow that created their possibility in long past ages. It is thus that nature works; forces of destruction everywhere; and then beauty more highly organised, more perfect life. If a glance back into ages so far away seems too great a demand on the imagination, go only over into Italy, when some great volcano like Vesuvius bursts into a fiery torrent, fills the sky with pall of black smoke, throws up rocks into the air that sear the flowers and the grass on which they fall, pours out white-hot torrents of lava that wither into one black ruin the works of man and of nature alike; and then a little later see again, and the lava has cooled into virgin soil, vines are growing where that fiery torrent fell, the huts of the cottagers, rose-covered, are dotted over the heaps that once were seething torrents of fiery lava, and nature is again laughing into beauty where there was only horror, stifling atmosphere, uproar, human and animal destruction everywhere.

For so it is that nature works. She is always working to ideal ends, to beauty, to harmony, to order. You cannot keep her ugly, mar her as you may. Cover her slopes with the slag of iron furnaces and make great heaps of refuse over the place where once the hawthorn was in bloom—never mind, a little later nature will be at work again, and the slag heaps will be turned into green sloping fields, and the piles of refuse will be covered with grass and flowers. She finds a ruin and she covers it till it is verdant with the leaf of the creeper. She takes a dung-heap and changes it into the playful tendrils of the vine. She is always bringing beauty out of ugliness, order out of disorder, harmony out of chaos. You think it but the blind working of unconscious forces, but does not so settled a plan, so definite a continued regeneration, speak rather of intelligences who are artists in their conceptions and who realise the laws of beauty, with ever-fecund imagination, producing the exquisite and the perfect? And so it is in the outer nature.

But let us now rather turn towards Man, and see whether in the outer phenomena of human history we can trace anything like a plan which is working for the perfect evolution of man. Now for this purpose you must read history over wide areas of time and vast extents of country. Let me lead you to one interesting succession that you can trace through historic times, in which you will see West and East, East and West, invading and conquering each other, and the great sceptre of empire going as by the swing of a pendulum from one side to the other. You see as you look back into the dawn of history the mighty western empire, the Toltec, which existed where now the waves of the Atlantic roll, which stretched out one hand and laid it on Mexico, and the other hand and rested it upon Ancient Egypt, one of the very mightiest empires the world has ever known. Then as you come down in history, empire leaves the West, and empire after empire rises up in the East, and Asia is the seat of power, and the sceptre of supremacy is wielded by her hand. Follow the course of history, and again the sceptre of empire swings slowly over to the West. Greece rolls back Persia, and even passes eastwards and invades the northern parts of India. A little later, and Rome arises and Carthage rules, and the empire of the world again is centred in the West. Go on a little later, and again Asia takes up the imperial *rôle,* her hosts sweep over Europe, destroy the last ruins of the Roman Empire, and spread westward as far as France, until they are hammered back by Charles Martel, and the great wave of conquest recoils again to Asia. But she has not yet finished. From Arabia the Moors spread along Africa, and conquer Southern Spain; from Syria and the northern parts of Asia Minor the Turkish hosts sweep over South-eastern Europe, until they are turned back by Hunyadi Janos, and they remain in the south-eastern corner of Europe under the crescent banner of the Arabian prophet. Then Europe arises once again, and after a while she begins the invasion once more of Asia. Asia had conquered Europe, Europe now begins to conquer Asia; first in the quiet guise of commerce, and then, later, by invading armies. And now in our own days once more in the far East Japan has thrown her sword into the scale of empire, and it is beginning to weigh down again in Asia, and the end has not yet come. Is there nothing to learn from that strange swinging backwards and forwards, eastward and westward, no plan, no working for human evolution, no profit out of all these great invasions and tremendous outpourings of human blood? When we look at the results we see that every invasion has enriched the invaded people, every conquest has left the conquered with something that before they did not enjoy. When the Moors conquered Spain they brought Science back with them, and Science continued to spread over the whole of Europe although the Moors were driven out of Spain. And so, when the Crusaders went into Asia, the Saracens taught those warriors the art of chivalry, and the Crusaders, on the other hand, taught to the too haughty and indifferent East the immeasurable value of self-sacrifice. And everywhere you see the same. East and West are different; and therefore it is necessary that they should come into contact, conquer each other, invade each other, and with each swing of the pendulum give something of East to West, or something of West to East, until both great types are blended in the perfect man and the evolution of humanity, perfect in all its possibilities, shall be with us. Thus we read the changes in history and the continual shifting destinies of human kind, the mighty power behind the outward phenomena, the successful conquests, the changing scale of empire, altering ever, changing ever, but all co-operating to the final goal of man.

And if instead of those vast changes, instructive as they are, you try to look behind the veil of the history of one country, can you not see in national as well as in international history the working out of definite causes, turned deliberately to aims to be achieved? The various passions of men, their ambitions and their hatreds, their jealousies and their conquests, all are brought into the one great current which works for human good; a real alchemy, a mighty transmutation, in which all the baser metals are turned to gold, the pure gold of a perfect man. Let us look for a moment and see whether we can trace the action of any great Powers in the stories of individual nations, and whether they do not become a little more intelligible by thus looking behind the veil. Now it is a very old Christian belief, taken by Christians originally from the Jews, that every nation has its own angel-king or angel-guardian. You find many a hint of it in the Hebrew and the Christian Bibles. Origen, of whom I spoke the other night, was so wise and so learned that the smaller men who followed did not understand him; he was too great an occultist to be readily understood by smaller minds, and he thus escaped canonisation at the hands of the Church. That great thinker, Origen, has a very interesting chapter on the part played by the angels of nations in the changing affairs of men, and he points out, what many of you may have noticed in the Hebrew Old Testament, that that which is often ascribed to the direct action of God, and so becomes grotesque, is rational if it is looked at from the standpoint of a great, though limited, superhuman Intelligence. And he alleges, though the allegation may seem a little startling nowadays to some of you, that the Hebrew Word which is translated "the Lord" in the earlier Hebrew books is not the word which is translated "God," and that the word which is translated "the Lord" should be translated "the Angel of Israel;" and he points to one verse in the Book of Judges, which has been a very useful weapon in the hands of those who have assailed Christianity, and it is a very peculiar verse: "The Lord was with Judah, and He drave out the inhabitants of the mountain, but could not drive out the inhabitants of the valley because they had chariots of iron." Now, it is a very peculiar thing, if you change the words "the Lord" into the word "God," that God was with Judah, and that He could manage the inhabitants of the mountain, but not those of the valley; but if you make it the "angel-guardian" you can realise quite well that that verse might be true without any stretch of probability; for such rulers are limited in power though greater than we are, and where they are pitted the one against the other, in attack or in defence of their own peoples, then comparatively small things may turn the scale. But to bring supreme power in on one side and then have it checkmated by chariots of iron is absurd, and you cannot wonder that many a freethinker has picked out that verse and held it up in mockery to show how childish were the ideas held by the ancient Jews. And so you may find other verses which, if you translate them according to the idea of Origen, become intelligible to those who know anything about the working of unseen intelligences. But if you make a world in which on one side there is a Supreme Being, and on the other human beings, and nothing between, you have an unintelligible cosmos, irrational and impossible to understand. And so in all the different religions of other nations you find the same idea about the angel-ruler, or guardian of the nation, taking part in the national affairs. If you go to Roman history you find Castor and Pollux in the ranks of the Romans. If you go to Grecian history, you find the Goddess Minerva or the God Hermes taking part in the battles of their people. If you go to the Norsemen you find Odin fighting with his favourite heroes. Go to India, and you find exactly similar legends there about the mingling of these invisible beings in the struggles and combats of their nations. And so in all the religions of the world you have testimony to the same thing. Look for a moment at the history of the Indian nation, and see how strangely you may trace in that the working of what seems a plan for the benefit of man. There was a time in India when you had a marvellous civilisation, when you had mighty kings, powerful rulers, when you may read how all the nations around, even from the far-western peoples, brought tributes to the mighty kings of that ancient land. You find her mighty in war as well as in the arts of peace. You find amongst her population the fighting class who ringed her around with a wall of steel, so that none might be able to invade; and then, as you trace her history down, you find that some 5000 years ago, as Indian story tells, there was a great manifestation of divine power; how one set of Indian people was put against another in sharp antagonism by the direct action of these great beings; how they fought the one against the other, slaying and being slain, until the

Indian sword was broken and her warriors were too few to guard her great frontiers. From that time onwards, from that great battle raging for 18 days till the opposing armies were well-nigh exterminated, you can trace her history downwards by invasion after invasion. Her walls were broken, her rich lands lay open, her people could no longer defend themselves, and invader after invader swept over that once mighty land. The Mussulmans came, army after army, and for a thousand years they fought and conquered and ruled. Then one European nation after another began to make inroads along her borders, leased pieces of land, built warehouses here and there; Dutch, Portuguese, French, all tried their hands on India, until at last the English merchants came. You may trace their history; how they begged and borrowed and stole, increasing continually their possessions; how they made treaties and broke them; how they took lands to guard and kept them, and so gradually partly by force, partly by fraud, partly by the treachery of Indian against Indian, they built up that mighty dependency of England in Asia that you know as the Indian Empire.

Now what is there in that strange succession of events which seems to some of us significant as to the part which India has played and has to play in the world? The English people found, when they got the upper hand and began to settle and to study the people among whom they came, a mighty literature; they found a marvellous philosophy; they found drama that was old when their own nation was still in a state of savagery; they found a philosophy so wonderful that modern Europe has gone into ecstacies over it, and declares it sublimer and loftier and grander than anything else the world has known; a philosophy that was the parent of Greek thought, that was brought from India into Greece, a philosophy that within the limits of this nation for many an age was closed in and kept, a priceless heritage, a wondrous treasure, not meant for India alone, but for the helping of the world. But it could not have become a world-possession if she were to have been able to guard herself always and shut herself in against the countries around her. Her warriors were exterminated that she might be conquered and that many nations might find their homes within her borders; and when the English came, the English who are building up the mightiest of all the Empires of the world, the English whose language is becoming the world-language, and is girdling the whole globe with one intelligible tongue, they came and conquered and held where all other Europeans had failed; and Indian Scriptures, Indian philosophy, Indian drama, translated into the universal English tongue, are now vitalising the religion of the conquerors, fertilising their fields of thought. No other race could have done it; no other language would have worked in the same way; no other nation could have wrought the same effect. And now those gems of Indian literature are becoming familiar all the world over, familiar as the writings of our own poets, familiar as the teachings of our own philosophers. And sometimes a nation is set apart like that, kept for a while encircled with a wall that cannot be over-climbed until she has grown great and strong and full of loftiest thought; and then her border is broken down, her land taken, and her people subjugated, in order that the treasures there accumulated may become the world's wealth and possession, common instead of national property, taking their part in the helping of the world.

There is another nation nearer home to you—the Irish people. There is another people whose destiny is strange, and at first it might seem almost unintelligible, just as it might have seemed strange and unintelligible that the great Eastern civilisation should have sunk down and become subjected. For the Irish people are a strange and peculiar people, a very different type of temperament from the conquering English race, who are Teutons for the most part. Teutonic in brain are the English; scientific, skilful in all application, clear in their thought, and practical in their application. The Irishman is not so; he is poetic, excitable, utterly different in temperament and type from the Englishman, the Keltic brain being opposed in character to the Teutonic. Ireland has had a fate something like that of India; conquered and held in subjection. Most of you probably know the sad story of Ireland's past. You know the way in which her manufactures were crushed out, in order that the manufactures of England might hold the markets of the world, just as Indian manufactures have been destroyed in order that Lancashire and Manchester might flourish. You know how the unfair restrictions on Ireland's exports made her manufactures impossible, so that they utterly perished. You know how her population diminished because the land could not support the population that land and manufactures together had kept in prosperity. You know how bitter penal laws crushed the life out of the great majority of the Roman Catholic people of the country, and how the Protestant supremacy forced upon them conditions which made life impossible, impoverishing the masses of the people; you know the hatred that grew up out of it, the hatred that still is struggling against the English yoke, and the memory of wrong, not forgotten by those who suffered, which makes the gulf of hatred still between the two Islands which make up the empire at home. And you know how in our own time efforts have been made; you saw how Parnell rose, the strange rise of a strong, powerful man; you know how he was not strong enough to do his work to keep his people from crime, and how he was broken and fell. But still that same country is kept separate; still walled round, as it were, apart from the empire, and a menace to it. Do you never ask why? Have you never tried to understand the purpose? Does it never strike you that perchance in that Keltic people there are possibilities of spiritual life which may come back in richest blessings to England, to Europe, as gradually her people rise out of the dreamy legendary fancies of the past, and take up the spiritual heritage which is within their reach, which is born, as it were, in their blood? For what India is to Asia, Ireland is to Europe; mystical, with the religious instinct woven into the hearts of her people; Ireland is the religious teacher of the future in Europe, as India is and has been the religious teacher of the world; alike in their isolation, alike in their subjugation, alike in the power of their spiritual thought, Ireland is a western India, India an eastern Ireland. And from those two poles, both within the British Empire, shall spread from east to west, and from west to east, the fertilising flood of religion which shall gradually raise the whole of the empire to a loftier spiritual level. Now look again for a moment at that Indian people, and see how evil things work for good. You read now of much unrest in India; you read of a national movement and all the rest of it; probably you have not troubled yourselves to trace the way in which that movement has gradually arisen. India was asleep, almost dead, as far as any love of country in her people, any sense of nationality, was to be found. Her spiritual life was gradually vanishing, her peculiar type was being gradually taken away from the treasures that have to enrich humanity. You sent her a Ruler, powerful and strong; but a ruler without sense of eastern feeling, without knowledge, the real knowledge, that comes from sympathy with eastern ways; before he came, some of her own people had been preaching to her of possible greatness. You had fed them on English literature; you had taught them of the English constitutional struggles for freedom; you had preached in your schools and colleges the grandeur of English liberty and the greatness of the English people; and the Indians are of the same race as you are, an older family of the same great Aryan race. They naturally assimilated your ideals and the story of your struggles, and some at least were fired with the longing for constitutional liberty. But the mass of the people cared nothing for these things; the great mass of the people were utterly indifferent, and the voices of those who spoke were voices crying in the wilderness. Then came your strong ruler, the Viceroy before the present one, with his Universities' Commission and his Education Act, under the plea of raising Indian education; he made it so costly that it was utterly beyond the reach of the class which has not only learning as its birthright, but has poverty as well. For in India the learned are poor and the learned class is a poor class; and by making education expensive he left it open to the rich and ignorant, but shut out the learned and the poor. As soon as the Universities Act was made the law of the land, India began to stir from her slumber of ages, for she cared much for learning though she had lost the care for rule. She desired to know; this was instinctive in her, for thousands of years she had sought knowledge, and so the people unmoved before began to move, and they began to say: "We must educate ourselves; and if education is to be made costly so that we cannot have it, by our rulers, then we will have our own national education, and train our own sons and educate our own people, and we will not be dependent on these English Universities, but we will guide our own education and take it into our own hands." And that was the first thrill of national life that passed through India, that determination to have education for herself. And there was another great movement in India; I myself have been preaching it for the last 14 years there; an economic movement, trying to persuade Indians to make their own goods and wear their own productions, telling them it was not worth while to grow cotton and send it to Lancashire to be woven into cloth and then sent back and sold in India, thus destroying the old weaving, industry indigenous to that great continent advising them to follow their own arts rather than the arts of the west, to produce their own exquisite manufactures instead of bad copies of Western goods; but nobody listened very much and nobody cared. They saw their weaving industry was perishing, they saw the weavers leaving the looms by which they could no longer live and crowding the already overcrowded agricultural population, and so making famine more inevitable than before. But they were asleep, they would not move. Then followed that great blessing in disguise to India, which caused her to make a political move. You have heard of the partition of Bengal; it was that which aroused one part of the Indian people into fury, and they took up the economic movement as a weapon of political warfare, and the result has been that it has spread from one part of the country to the other, and India is now returning to its proper economic position; hence the manufactures of India are improving, and the powers of the Indians are being turned again to art and crafts and manufactures, and they are beginning to lay the foundation of wealth and prosperity for their own country. That which was supposed to take away from them even the liberty they had has been turned into a great enfranchising movement, and so is building up the India of the future to be a nation in the great Federation of free nations into which the British Empire shall evolve. And in that way what seemed most evil has turned to most good, for the unrest is passing, but the great wave of national life, *that* will endure. Out of that there shall come new knowledge and new power to this great federation of free peoples, and the India that otherwise might have remained asleep has been aroused by scourge because she would not be aroused by precept; her invisible Ruler has forced her into activity, since she was too fast asleep to be moved by words alone.

Look at Russia. There is a country that has a future before it, but through what a hell of suffering is she being guided to her future greatness. A wonderful people is that Russian people. I do not know how far you may have cared to interest yourselves in that great movement made now many, many years ago, a movement without parallel, I think, in the histories of nations, where the young of the Russian nobility, sons and daughters of the noble houses of Russia, fired with the love of humanity, compassionate, with a desire to help the miserable, starving people, toilers, peasants, manufacturing slaves in most miserable and wretched conditions, left their homes, left their luxury, left their idle lives. Boys and girls of 16, 17, and 18 years of age, leaving their homes behind them, went out into the fields and factories, worked side by side with peasants in the fields, side by side with weavers and toilers in filthy factories, lived with them, worked with them, starved with them—and taught them. That was the first great movement; that was the first effort of this dawning Russian nation, a splendid example of self-sacrifice, the effort of the rich for the poor. On that came down the heavy hand of government and the crushing weight of tyrannic laws; those young ones who only meant to help found themselves seized and flung into prison untried. They found themselves sent to Siberia on charges of political agitation into which they had not entered; they found themselves plunged into the dungeon and exiled to the mines; they perished by scores, by hundreds, and by thousands; and it was out of the bitterness and anger which grew out of a ruthless persecution, that what is known as the Red Terror of Russia awakened; it was a movement of despair against intolerable oppression. But the yoke of government pressed heavily; the first effort had failed;

what was to be done? The nation was guided into a hopeless and desperate war; she sent out her children by the thousand across Asia to grapple with the far Eastern foe on her extreme borders. It was said that they "fought like lions, but were led by asses." They failed; they were beaten, crushed by their more capable enemy. But in that war much of the strength of the government was broken and a new movement for freedom became possible in Russia. And still she is writhing in the anguish of the birth of a new nation, still she is in misery and well nigh in despair, while the breath of freedom is blowing over her people; but out of that defeat and that misery, out of that revolution and that struggle a new Russia will be born, a Russia fit to take her place in civilisation. And out of her magnificent materials shall be builded a nation that shall be mystical in its tendency, idealistic in its aims, as well as mighty in its force. It is when you study history in this way and see how mighty a Power guides a nation through misery to happiness, that you begin to understand what is meant by the phrase "the Guardians of Humanity." See how, when a nation is to be used to help forward the race, how many able ones are born among her rulers; and when a nation has to learn her lessons in anguish, see how amid her leaders you find none who are fit to lead. You say it is all chance, that it all happens by accident, that there is no plan, no guiding, no arrangements, that all the results work out without any intelligence to plan, without any guidance to shape means to ends? If that be so in the world, then one might also imagine that any great work of human skill were likewise produced by blind unconscious laws. We know that human intelligence can plan and direct. Wherever we see a plan we take for granted that intelligence is behind it. And if in the study of history we can see this plan among the nations, this shifting of empire, the guidance of peoples to greatness, the casting down of some and the lifting up of others, the leading of the nations through misery to freedom and through struggle to peace, is it so strange to look behind the outer phenomena and to seek for the Intelligences that guide? And so we see in all these strifes and upheavals among the nations the workings of the world-process, whereby a perfect humanity shall develop; in all the struggles a foreseen end; in all the sufferings a lesson to be learned and an achievement to be made.

And looking thus at history it becomes intelligible; thus studying it we can see as it were the outline of the plan shining through the mass of the details, and we begin to realise that men may co-operate therein, may learn the laws, and then be able to utilise them, and that just as in your smaller contacts with nature you study her in order to find out the underlying principles which guide, and, knowing them, use them to bring about that which you desire, so in the larger history of mankind and in the story of the nations you may find by study the principles upon which they are being builded, and learn that the old prophet did not speak wrongly when he declared that righteousness exalteth a nation, and that those who follow righteousness shall win peace and prosperity.

And those other Great Ones that I spoke of under the general name of Masters—They have to do with the religious evolution of man, his spiritual unfolding, even as the angel-rulers I have spoken of have to do with the outer destinies of nations. We mean by the word "Master" one who founds a great religion, gives a new form to the everlasting verities, clothes them in a shape congenial to the time and to the customs and temperament of the people, gives the particular garb which will suit them and help them along the path of their evolution. Again glance over history, and you will find one law continually showing itself out; whenever there is to be a new step forward in the evolution of mankind, whenever a new civilisation is to be born, a new policy to be shaped, then a fresh spiritual impulse comes to the world, and some great religious teacher appears in the world to give a new form to religion, a form which shall dominate the coming civilisation. Over and over again in the past you find it; Egypt built its polity on a religious foundation, and its Pharoah was the highest priest as well as the ruler of the State; the whole of the Indian polity is based on a religious foundation; Syria the same, as also Persia. Before the Christ was born, the great outline of Grecian philosophy had been brought from India and Egypt; Rome had been built on her own great faith; and the Christ was born before the new Western Civilisation, the Teutonic, began. Christianity is but the last but one of the great religions of the world, born to build a new civilisation, or, if you prefer it, to be the Mother on whose bosom that infant civilisation should be nursed. Look through Europe and see how it has dominated all the thought of Europe; her greatest literature has grown from the religious stem; her most splendid art has been inspired by her faith; her marvellous architecture is the outcome of her religion. Religious thought has embodied itself in her literature, her art, and her architecture. But that is nothing new, it has always been so. Thus whenever you get the first striking of the note of religion by a Master, then follows the birth of a new civilisation dominated by the form He gave; and over the world to-day you are seeing the spread of a new spiritual wave, a new impulse of the ancient life; not only in that movement that we call the Theosophical Society, which is a small thing, but in that vast movement all the world over which is asserting itself in a dozen different forms, but of which the inner thought is identical throughout. It is the reaction against materialism; it is the re-assertion of the ideal as mightier than the material, of life as the master of matter. · You see it in the changing attitude of science of which I spoke, voiced by Sir William Crookes; you see it in the new impulse in art, which is turning from mere imitative production and again is striving after the ideal; you see it in literature, where idealism is also beginning to triumph; you see it even in the ordinary publications of the day, where the unseen and the invisible are beginning to play their part again, no longer ridiculed, but looked at with interest; you see it in the wave of psychic evolution which is showing itself in the most civilised nations; you see it in the growing vitality in the Christian Church, and in the new power of the mystic life which is beginning to again exercise its sway over men; you see it now approaching a more concrete form, in the Theosophical Society; but the new thought, the new feeling, the forms of fresh thinking that you see around you—they are all alike in principle, although differing in their wording and their outward shape. But this mighty movement is not going to make a new religion; it proclaims the unity of all religions, and the one spirit dominating the variety of forms; it does not seek to bring people into one Church or another; it does not look for converts from one faith to another; it says that all faiths are one in their essence, that all faiths are searchings after God, though in many ways and along many roads; it has as one of its mottoes those words which have been spoken under different forms by the great world Teachers: "Mankind comes to me along many roads, and on whatever road a man approaches me, on that road do I welcome him, for all roads are mine." That is the Voice of the Spirit sounding above the jar of contending faiths; that is the declaration of the inner unity despite the variety of outside ceremony and dogma; it is the declaration once more that as one Sun enlightens all the earth, so one Spirit and one Truth shine out in every nation for the illumination of human hearts and lives; it is the declaration of the brotherhood instead of the rivalry of religions; the proclamation of many mighty Masters who are all one Brotherhood, and who teach a common verity, a common reality, a common truth. And just as the one sunlight is broken up by the prism into the seven colours of the spectrum, so is the one white light of truth broken up by the prism of the human mind into the many colours of the various religions of the world; and as by putting another prism in the path of the coloured rays it re-combines them all into one, so, by placing the spiritual view of truth in the path that the differently coloured rays of the many religions make, you re-combine them all into one, and the white light of truth shines out once more. Religions have each their own characteristic, each their own special beauty, each teaching some great truth to the world; but all truths are fundamentally one, as all forces may be combined into one universal force. And so in the movement of to-day, instigated as ever by the Masters of the world religions, in that movement towards unity, that movement towards idealism, that movement that proclaims the spiritual nature of man—in that we may see the guiding hand of these human yet divine Guardians of Humanity, who are gathering together all nations and all religions into one mighty Brotherhood, in order that a civilisation of peace, a civilisation of love, a civilisation of international brotherhood, may bind together all the nations of the world in the one bond of humanity, and there can be no strangers, no outcasts, no foreigners among people who know humanity as one, and the nations as the organs of a single Body.

Nature's Finer Forces

Those of you who have kept at all abreast of the advances of modern science can hardly have avoided being struck by the very great change that has come over the attitude of Science during the last twenty years. In the days when many of you, and I, were young, Science was dealing with matter, with forms, with all these outer phenomena of nature that can be seen, can be heard, can be touched; and out of the study of these phenomena Science was led to believe in the existence of certain things that could not be seen, nor heard, nor touched. To all these invisible, inaudible, intangible things which caused movements in matter that were not otherwise intelligible, the name of force was given. Matter, it was said, was inert, could not move itself, could not stop itself if set going by something from outside. And it was pointed out in dealing with this inertia of matter that when it was made to move by what was called a force, and force was defined as that which causes movement in matter, it never stopped moving of its own accord, but only by something else that interfered, such as friction. As you know, in ordinary machinery, in the very common instance of the bicycle wheel, you judge the worth of the bearings of that bicycle wheel by the time that it will go on turning after a certain force has set it going. If it stops quickly you say the bearings are not good, too much friction; so thoroughly is it recognised that matter does not stop moving of itself, but is made to stop by something else, whether it be friction or any other cause. Out of this idea of the inertia of matter necessarily grows the co-relative idea of force, as that which causes motion or checks motion, and so Science built up a universe of the two, force and matter. These, of course, were abstractions taken in the singular, and we then have to deal with forces in the plural, the various kinds of things that cause motion in matter. There was, theoretically, one force which might take many shapes, as there was one matter which could assume many forms, and those are two of the fundamental conceptions of modern Science. In the days of which I speak, twenty, thirty years ago, nothing else was thought by many scientific men to be necessary in order to explain the happenings, the phenomena, of the universe. Matter and force, it was said, were enough for everything. The elder of you will remember the famous book, sometimes called the *Bible of Materialism*, by the great German Scientist, Büchner. In that book, under the title of *Force and Matter*, the writer dealt with the various phenomena of the world, how the changes took place, and how these, too, were to be considered. I need not remind you, save just in passing, of the definition that was then common for an atom. It was a particle of matter, and according to the author I have just mentioned and his view, which would have been endorsed by other scientists of his own time, the atom was infrangible. When you got down to the atom, you would come to the ultimate, to that which "cannot be cut." That was the notion that Science had at that time, the same idea that had been held for thousands of years, from the times of the great Greek scientists, and long before that. But in addition to that, it was laid down that this particle of matter which could not be further divided was also unchangeable in its properties. I remember well—for I translated Büchner's book into English—his positive statement that an atom of carbon to all eternity is an atom of carbon, that it has never been anything else, and so on—one phrase after another—showing you how deeply rooted in the minds of the scientists of that time was the conception of an unchangeable atom, which possessed definite attributes, uncreated, indestructible, and that these atoms, with the co-relative force which gives motion, were the two things out of which the universe was built up. Science does not now take that position. One of our leading scientists, Sir Oliver Lodge, wrote a very admirable book, well worthy of study, in which he says there is another factor in the universe—life; that you cannot identify life with force, as many of the older scientists did, regarding life as only the outcome of a particular arrangement of matter and inseparable from it, disappearing with a change in the arrangement, appearing with an arrangement capable of showing out that force. It would be worth the while of the more thoughtful thinkers among you to read his argument, for it is admirably put. He shows in that book that while matter and force make up the universe exterior to consciousness, you cannot regard consciousness as a kind of force, you cannot make life identical with a certain kind of force. Without going into all his arguments, I may put to you the one great fact generally, that force has no direction which is not imposed upon it—bursts out in all directions. It is only when mind comes in and makes a certain apparatus or mechanism that the force is directed in a particular way, as in a pistol or gun your gunpowder explodes, but in order that it may do so effectively, mind has had to contrive the tube of the pistol or the grooving of the gun. In this way force is utilised as well as matter by the overruling power of consciousness, of mind, and by very many arguments he buttresses up this statement—a fundamental statement—the one which sees nature not as a duality of force and matter, but as a trinity of matter, force, and mind. It is well to realise that very much of what I have to say to you has a bearing on this view.

But let me remind you, before I take that up, of another change that has come over Science; it used to argue to the existence of force, though invisible, because matter cannot move without it. It is now arguing for the existence of matter as a medium for force. That is, the whole thing is turned upside down. Instead of arguing that there must be an invisible, indestructible force, because matter moves, which otherwise would be moveless, Science now is arguing that we must have matter, for we know of forces and they are moving in something. So that you now deduce matter from force instead of force from matter—a very remarkable change, showing you the line upon which Science is travelling.

How has that change come about? Because science has been advaucing, step by step, from the coarse to the subtle, from the gross to the fine. First, examination was through the avenues of the senses—the eye, the ear, the tactile power. But in their investigations scientists found out that many things were existing which these senses were unable to cognise—things too small for the eye to see, things too far away for the eye to examine—and as they studied more and more closely they found that the human senses are things very limited in range, and that there are a vast number of vibrations that do not affect our senses at all, that to us had not existed because we are unable to answer them. Consequently, to try to improve the eye and make it more effective than otherwise it would be, to make the eye see what by itself it could not see, they invented the microscope, and raised it to power after power, until the very very minute becomes visible by the process of continually magnifying it, and thus raising it to a size which the human eye is able to perceive. So with regard to the infinitely great, as it is often called, the mighty Universe around us; as the eye could not see far enough, they made the telescope to assist it in plunging into the depths of space. The inventions of the microscope and the telescope are but an illustration of the method of science, climbing up step by step from the coarse to the fine. They made balances so delicate that an infinitesimal fraction of a grain would make a scale depressed, so delicate that they could measure weight to an almost inconceivable minuteness. As science went on conquering the worlds of nature, the worlds of matter and of force, it was by her apparatus that she made her conquests, and the invention of scientists was taxed to the utmost to make a better apparatus, a more delicate piece of mechanism, some way of putting matter together in order that the mysteries of matter might be further investigated by man. But now she is coming to a very difficult place. She has gone beyond the region for her finest instruments. Her most exquisite apparatus no longer helps her in the realms into which she is penetrating. She wants to understand ether, and ether is imponderable by the finest of her balances. She has passed into a realm where the intangible, the invisible, the inaudible, are crowding around her on every side, and she dimly senses their presence, but is unable to perceive. What is she to do? Problem after problem remains unanswered because the means of investigation are no longer ready to her hand. She knows that there are things outside her ken. She has found it to be so even by making improvements in her machinery, and at last, almost in despair, she has had to turn to the one deductive science, mathematics, and she prays the mathematician to discover for her what the senses, however aided, are not able to observe. It is remarkable that mathematics is the one science in the modern world that works from generals to particulars by deduction, and is the only one which is absolutely sure. All others work by what is called induction, from particulars to generals. Induction is very sure if you have got hold of all the particulars, but the weakness of that method is that if you fail to observe any one particular, and leave it out, the whole of your investigation fails. That has been happening over and over again lately with modern Science. She has been discovering that in her inductions she has left things out which she had not observed, and has thus vitiated her conclusions. The conclusions have failed. Arguments which seemed unanswerable, conclusions that seemed irrevocable, have been knocked into pieces by discovering that something was left out, so that the induction failed, and Science is face to face now with all the difficulties she thought she had answered.

You know that there are many people who have a greater extent of sense perception as regards the ear, the eye, the sense of touch, than others. Some people can see more than others with regard to delicate shades of colour. If I took you over to Persia or to Kashmir, I could bring before you carpet makers who would see a dozen shades of colour where you and I see only one. Their eyes have been trained to see delicate shades which the ordinary eye looks at unperceiving, and the extraordinary richness of the Persian carpet, the one in which one shade melts into another, the delicacy of the Kashmir weaving, turn on this extraordinary delicacy of the Persian and Kashmirian eye. They see where we are blind, they see variety of colours where we see uniformity.

It is the same with the ear. Of Oriental music most Europeans say it is flat, but what is called flatness by the Western ear is due to gradations of sounds too fine for the ordinary Western ear to hear, and yields tones which are most exquisite to the trained sense. The Indian can discover delicate gradations of sounds produced by his instruments that are not perceptible to the ordinary European ear, trained to a different scale and to different kinds of sounds. But that is not the only thing that shows us that our powers as regards the senses differ very much one from the other. Any few of you, picked out at random, can hear notes of music, sounded out to you from what is called the siren, an apparatus which yields notes higher and higher, by vibrations of air, shorter and more rapid as it turns. At a certain point most would say that there was silence. You see the instrument whirling round, and say: "It is moving still, but there is no sound." There is really a higher sound, and one man perhaps will say: "I still hear it; it is very shrill." It gives a still higher note, and that man becomes deaf to the sound, and will only see the movement. Another, perhaps, will say: "I can still hear it." There is a very fine sound, until at last the notes grow so fine that no ordinary human ear can hear them at all; yet they are shrilling through the atmosphere; the vibrations are dashing up against your ear. You have reached the limit of your power of hearing. It is the same with colour. You can see only the seven colours of the spectrum, and all the varieties of colour coming between the violet and the red. But there are vibrations below the red. Science has found them out, and by changing their rate of vibration has brought them within the limit of radiance. There are vibrations beyond the violet. Photographs are chiefly made by what are called the actinic rays, which no human eyes can perceive unaided, but there are certain chemicals which can be put on a sheet so that beyond the violet or purple, you can see the faint purplish hue which tells you of vibrations too delicate for your eye to catch unaided. All these things go to show that you are in a universe of endless possibilities, and you can only know that to which you are able to answer. You know in the Universe of matter that which you can reproduce, and nothing more. All around you finer and more subtle vibrations are playing upon you. You are absolutely insensitive to them. You have developed no organ which is able to answer them, and hence for you they do not exist. These vibrations have colour beyond the spectrum scale of colour. They are there, but you cannot see them. The vibrations of sound are beyond the octaves of sound. They are there, but you cannot hear them. And so Huxley said truly that if our ears were finer we could hear the sap moving in the trees, and the growing of the grass by the side of the road. There are sounds everywhere, inaudible; sights everywhere, invisible; vibrations everywhere, intangible; and a marvellous universe, which would become more marvellous, if only our senses were finer to answer to it, if only we could develop powers that as yet humanity has not normally evolved. Sir William Crookes has helped us here, and has pointed out, making a table of vibrations, all the vibrations that he regards as present in the Universe of matter; in that table he has marked out what we know of the groups of vibrations: that there are electrical vibrations, sound vibrations, a gap, vibrations of light, another gap, and so on, showing how much we know not, how little comparatively we know. Then he went on to say (and we must remember that Crookes is a Theosophist, who studies from the standpoint of the finer universe) that possibly these finest vibrations in the ether might be the vibrations by which thought is transferred from brain to brain without the medium of coarser matter, beyond the ordinary methods of communication, and he suggested whether it is not possible that some organ will evolve—rudimentary at present in most, but comparatively active in some —whereby the subtle vibrations of ether-transmitted thought may pass from one to another without the grosser matter. Elsewhere he pictured the universe as it would be if your eyes and mine answered to electrical waves instead of to waves of light. Everything would change. Standing here, if my eyes answered to electricity instead of to light, I could not see you, but when I looked through the wall I should be able to see right into the street; for the electrical currents could pass through the walls, and if my eyes answered to them the wall would be to me transparent as glass, but dry air is a non-conductor of electricity, and if the air between you and me is dry enough, we should be invisible to each other if we saw by electrical waves instead of by light waves. He pointed out that if we looked along a silver wire in dry air, we should see a tunnel through the darkness, the air opaque, the wire transparent. He told us a number of other things of that sort, which would make the world quite different from the present.

It is at the point of the discovery of those finer worlds that Eastern Science, older by thousands of years than her Western sister, can give suggestions which perhaps the Westerner may not be too proud presently to utilise, for the Eastern Scientist has gone on quite different lines. What is his view of man? for it all turns upon that. He regards man as a spiritual intelligence, and he regards matter and force as of one nature, into which that spiritual intelligence comes, in order to study and know it. He does not confuse matter and spirit. Man is the living spirit, and his three great attributes are will, activity, and the power to know. And these three attributes of the spiritual intelligence are used in relation to matter and force, which are essentially one. Then our Eastern Scientist says that this spiritual intelligence takes on matter, and makes out of it what we call bodies, in order that he may come into touch with the various worlds of the material universe. As he puts on a certain kind of matter, he can learn about and investigate all things which are made up out of that kind of matter. It is the same idea, if you notice, that Science has, that you can only know a thing when you can answer it in yourself. But the Eastern thinker says that you have appropriated the matter, and have built it into suitable forms. The ordinary scientist will acknowledge that of the physical body, putting it in a different way. But the Eastern sage goes much further. He says: "You have appropriated every kind of matter in the universe, not only that of the physical universe around you; and as you have a physical body by which you can know a physical universe, so you have bodies of finer matter by which you may know finer worlds; you are normally in touch with three different worlds: the matter of your physical body brings you into touch with the physical world, and the matter of what we call the astral body, or part of the subtler body, brings you into touch with the desire world, and still finer matter, mental matter, brings you into touch with the world of mind.

And then he goes a step further. He says that as you have evolved your physical body, and by that evolved body contact the physical world, so you are evolving further finer bodies, and as you evolve them, you will contact the finer worlds; as you evolve them you will answer to the finer forces, and slowly and gradually you will, in process of evolution, be able to know worlds of finer matter and finer forces, in exactly the same way that you now know the world of gross matter and gross forces, that you call the physical universe. That is his view of bodies and worlds. With that theory, what would naturally be his practice? Where the Western scientist has made apparatus outside him, the Eastern scientist constructs apparatus inside him. That is the difference. Instead of making microscope and telescope and balances, he works to develop finer bodies, and so obtains a means of contact with the finer worlds. He declares that this is possible, and he tells you how to do it, and he bids you make your own experiments and try it for yourself. He points out to you, as I shall be pointing out to you when I deal with that question, that thought has created the physical organs in which it works, and that similarly it can create finer organs for finer purposes, subtler instruments for the measuring of subtler forces. Now I do not ask you to accept that as true, for the moment, but I do ask you is it so irrational, or is it not in consonance with what you already know of nature and of evolution?

Your physical eye has grown up to be what it is by a long process of evolution, going on for thousands, millions, of years. Your eye began in a little tiny speck of colour in the body of a jellyfish, which only knew a little change of light and darkness, distinguished dimly between the light and the dark. Imagine the feelings of other jellyfish, if they were able to reason as you can reason, if some adventurous jellyfish had pushed on the development of that little speck, and came back presently to his fellow jellyfish, and said: "It is quite possible to see a great many things that you can't see. I can see all sorts of things running about. I can see all sorts of creatures running around us, and can run away if they want to eat me." They would all say:

"What nonsense this audacious jellyfish is talking. How can he see when we can't see? How can he know when we, the wise and orthodox jellyfish, know nothing? What is all this nonsense he is talking about forms and things of this sort? How can we possibly escape when the moment comes for us to die? How can we see when anything is coming, and run away? If he is not a lunatic, he is a fraud, and is trying to get the better of us," and so on. These obstinate jellyfish go on in their own way until nature forces them to evolve. It is very much the same with all of you with your present powers. You can go on if you like, and slowly, slowly, nature will carry you onwards, until your psychical body has organs as your physical body has organs, and reveals to you a new world of wonderful phenomena that you can study as you study the phenomena of the physical world. But suppose you say: "I will learn by the experience of the past. I see that all these senses have been gradually evolved. I see that the eye has grown through all these stages in an immense evolution. I also notice that when we understand the laws of nature, and begin to work with them, they are our helpers. By them we can evolve very much more quickly. We are not at the head of evolution. Humanity has not yet reached perfection. Why should not I try to evolve a little more quickly by utilising the laws of nature that I know, and thereby increase the speed of evolution for myself and for my fellow men?" That is what is being done all round us with regard to the breeding of animals. How is it that a scientific breeder can, in the course of a few generations, develop in his stock certain characteristics? Because he knows the laws of nature and utilises those that suit him, and neutralises those that don't suit him. In that way he brings about what he desires very much more rapidly. By making intelligence a factor, you can do the same with your mind. The laws of psychology are fairly well known; the way in which the mind develops is fairly well understood. If you deliberately apply psychological laws to your own mind, intelligently, rationally, and persistently, you can evolve it at a pace which leaves behind ordinary evolution. Now, mind is the power that shapes matter. You shape your physical body from the subtler world which interpenetrates the physical. You can shape your subtle body and give it the organs whereby it shall contact the subtle worlds.

Meditation is the great way of doing this, and it is by meditation that the Eastern psychologist has developed senses which are able to answer to finer vibrations, which are able to contact things invisible to the physical eye. It is on these invisible things, of course, that all religions are really based, only that they have lost the methods of proving them, of demonstrating them to a sceptical world. The result has been that while those great truths—survival after death, communication with the other worlds, living the heavenly life while still in the physical body—are taught by religions, the method of proving them has been lost. Therefore, when Science challenges them with its experiments, they are obliged to say: "We can't demonstrate our truths to you in a similar way." They feel that they are right; a subtle instinct makes them cling to those ideas, despite all the arguments of Science, but they cannot prove them

Now, it is just here that Theosophy comes in, bringing some of the old Eastern knowledge within the power of study of the Western peoples, advising them to take up some of its methods if they would know the reality of the things in which they have been instructed, and so be able to face a sceptical world, and prove them by first-hand experiment, and not as simply stated on authority.

Let us see whether we cannot make out a good case for the belief in the finer sight, the finer hearing, the finer forces. Men like Frederick Myers came definitely to the conclusion that we are in touch with more worlds than one. You may remember that in "Human Personality," a most valuable book to read, he drew a distinction between what he called planetary consciousness, that which we are using every day, and cosmic consciousness, which touches the realities on which religions are based. Western science is being forced into this position now. It cannot escape it. It has found by its own experiments that there are forces subtler than those it is dealing with in the laboratory, forces that it cannot deal with by its apparatus. Psychologists cannot escape from contacting these things through human brains and human intelligences a little out of the normal. Some abnormal human brains have shown a greater capacity than normal brains to respond to finer vibrations. I will ask you for a moment to attend to that, for it is a point of enormous importance. When you deal with consciousness, you may deal with normal consciousness as you see it all round you, the consciousness of the market place and of the professional man, that by which you and I and all the folk around us communicate with each other. There is no doubt about that primary fact. We all know it. But you have not understood human consciousness, if you deal only with the consciousness that shows through the waking brain of ordinary people. The worlds of sleep and dreams were the next that Science tried to examine. First by trying to work upon the dream state by outside contact. You can read a good deal about that in Du Prel's "Philosophy of Mysticism." You can experiment, if you like, for yourselves, if you will take the trouble and have the patience. It has been shown that by touching the body in various ways you can produce dreams. One famous experiment which was made in France was touching the back of the neck of the sleeper, and wakening the sleeper by the touch. Between the time of the touch and the wakening—a fraction of a second—the man had dreamt a long story of how he had committed a murder, how he had been tried for the crime, heard the charge of the judge to the jury, been condemned to death for the murder, carried to the condemned cell, kept there till the day of the execution, brought out to the execution, and guillotined. As the knife touched his neck—the touch which started the dream—he woke. Now, that is one of many cases showing that the dream consciousness works much more rapidly than the waking consciousness, and therefore, works in finer matter than the waking consciousness. The rate of vibration in nervous matter we know, the nervous vibrations in the brain that correspond with waking thoughts. It has been measured; but if you can crowd the events of a week, of a month, of a year, into one part of a second of mortal time, it means that the vibrations corresponding with them are very much quicker, and would have to be measured by an entirely different law of space and time. That showed the scientific men that there was matter finer than that which they knew, and forces subtler than the forces they had studied. Soon they were not content with working under the old methods; they tried to catch and question the dreamer while he was still dreaming, and threw him into a trance that they might do so. So they used the finer forces of nature without understanding them; for when this eye is so closed in the hypnotic trance that it is incapable of receiving an impression, when, if you throw an electric light into it, there is no movement to close the pupil, then, though the eye is thus absolutely insensitive to light, the man can see much further than he can see through his physical eye. He can see hundreds of miles, can tell you what is happening far away; can see through a closed door, and describe what is taking place on the other side of it. People sometimes say this is mental telepathy. Let me give you an instance and see whether telepathy will explain this far sight, which can be used at a distance of hundreds of miles. You have all heard of my friend, the late Charles Bradlaugh. He was a materialist, and did not believe in these subtler things at all, but he was a man of extraordinary magnetic power and made a number of experiments in mesmerism. He gave it up because it seemed to have no natural explanation, and he had not the time to make sufficient investigations. One experiment he had made baffled him to the end. He used to experiment by mesmerising his wife. He told me the story himself. One day, in Leeds, I think, he mesmerised her, and said: "Go to the London office of the 'National Reformer,' and tell me what article they are setting up." In a moment she said: "I am there. Mrs. —— is setting up type." "All right," said he, "look at her, and see and read what she is setting up." His wife began to read the sentence that was being set up by the printer at the moment. She said: "The stupid woman, she has put a letter in upside down." Next morning the proof was delivered to him in Leeds, and he found the sentence his wife had read the day before, with the reversed letter that she had seen put in upside down in the setting of the type. There was certainly no telepathy there; it is not a case you can explain by telepathy, for he did not know it, she did not know it. They were not in touch with the people who were setting up the type. This case is valuable, inasmuch as it showed the accuracy of that far seeing, and was in itself so trivial. And you can take hundreds of cases of that sort, or experiment yourself if you want to find out about it. Such sight is a simple seeing in finer matter; nothing more, nothing miraculous, nothing super-human, only a finer organ of vision utilised by the same perceptive power that you use with the coarser organ of vision that you call your physical eye. We call it the astral eye. We call it astral sight. All men will have it after a time. In the long course of evolution, everyone will develop that keener power, and it is very interesting to notice that numbers of people are developing it now, and especially under certain conditions. We find more children born every year with that faculty. In the Western States of America, such as California or Kansas, large numbers of people are somewhat clairvoyant. What is the explanation of people being born with that keener, subtler, vision? One explanation of why so many are being born there with the finer vision is largely climatic. The climate is very different from the climate in Europe, and, I understand, from the climate here. The electric tension is very much higher; the air is filled with electricity to an enormous extent. It is so charged with electricity that if in the winter, when it is cold, you rub your feet on the carpet you can then put out your finger and light the gas. You often see that done as an experiment when, in a lecture on electricity, a person is put on an insulated seat and then is charged with electricity. But in these States no insulation is necessary, and it is a favourite game with little children, rubbing their feet on the carpet as they run, and then making sparks. I have seen it done over there, and have done it myself. You may say: "Why should that make a person clairvoyant?" The electrical condition puts the nerves into a state of higher tension, and they vibrate at a quicker rate. It is quite simple. That is not the only reason. There are other reasons, a number of other things that contribute. But there is one experiment any one of you might make which will show you how very little is the difference between the ordinary sight and the lower types of the keener sight. I have known people who, when they are ill, become clairvoyant. The answer is that their nerves are out of order, and at a greater tension than it is healthy for the nerves to be. You may say: "Well, then, it is largely the result of disease at present." There comes in the point of the abnormal. As I have said before, that which is abnormal to-day is not necessarily diseased. It may be a case of advancing evolution. There are two forms of nervous instability. One is the instability of degeneration, on the line of disease; the other is the instability of the growth of a higher sensitiveness, which means advance in evolution. You know how Lombroso and others of his school declared that all cases of genius were cases of degeneration, how they said that genius and lunacy were so closely allied that genius was a disease. Now, if it were true, in a way it would not matter, because everybody would rather have that disease than be without it. One's great longing would be to become diseased, if genius could only be had along that line, for after all one genius is worth a thousand ordinary people to the world. When Lombroso went on to say that all religions, all art, all prophecy, and so on, were all the results of diseased nerves, one felt inclined to go down on one's knees to pray that that disease might spread, for these are the things that make the world worth living in. Now what is the real explanation of this? It is true that these things are abnormal at present. I think we may put it in this way: in both cases the matter of the brain is in a state of what is called unstable equilibrium, and therefore easily thrown off its balance. As just said, there are two sorts of this instability, one of the instability which goes on into disease and madness; the other of the instability which evolves upwards to a higher stage of human evolution. One goes down into sub-consciousness; the other climbs up into super-consciousness. The man of genius shows you what the human race shall be. He is the prophecy of the future. He is not the product of degeneracy. He shows us what all men shall become at a stage of higher evolution. He is the high-water mark of human progress, and not the sign of a descent. There is, however, much to justify what Lombroso said. It is only fair to admit that at the present time the genius, the artist of the highest kind, the great religious leader, the seer, the prophet, the revealer, has often a brain too delicate to bear the rough vibrations of the outer world as it is constituted to-day. His brain is finer, but is often thrown out of tune, and the result is that side by side with the higher results of consciousness—the answering to the finer forces of the invisible world—you get what is called hysteria, the result of the overstrained condition of the nerves. There is no use in denying the facts. Can they be avoided? Yes. That is the answer of the Eastern scientist. He will say, as Lombroso says, that if you go with an unprepared body to receive these finer forces, they will jangle your nerves out of tune, they will trouble your brain and shatter your nervous system. But there is no reason why you should do it with an unprepared brain or body. Train your brain by strenuous thinking, by devotion to great ideals. Make your brain sensitive to the higher vibrations. But do it gradually. Go step by step. Evolve it slowly and constantly, and then you will be able to receive the finer forces without shattering the instrument whereby they become manifest to your intelligence. Along that line evolution will come. You can train yourself to receive the finer forces, and yet keep the body healthy. You must refine the body, train it to a finer sensitiveness, at the same time that you preserve perfect health. That is the training by which the finer forces will become your servants, while at the same time they shall not be allowed to disorganise the nervous system, now suited only for the lower forces and coarser types of matter. Along that line, then, human evolution will go, and you may gradually and slowly build up bodies, developing your astral organs and interlinking them with the physical, so that you may consciously live in more worlds than one, so that you may know that death is nothing except the passing through a doorway from one room into another. For as these senses develop, you will find that the people you call dead are not dead at all. They are more alive than they ever were, living in bodies of finer matter, learning to utilise finer forces. I do not mean that you should reach them by bringing them down here by materialisation, and cross-examining them. I mean that you should reach them by refining yourself, so that you can use the finer body that they wear, and mingle with them in the body that is yours as much as theirs, for you also have astral bodies. You are using them all the time. The only thing you have to do is to assist their evolution, to organise them, to shape the various organs which then will answer to the vibrations outside of finer worlds. Your friends who have passed through death are only living in the intermediate world first, and then in the heavenly. They are about you, and it is only a question of how much you can communicate with them by means of the finer matter which is part of you now, only you have not learnt to use it. As I said, all men will grow to it in time. It is yours, if you will, to grow to it more quickly. As you evolve by definite gradations you become more and more sensitive to the finer forces of the subtler world. If this be true, and many of us have proved it to be true by our own experience, Science may begin to utilise these things. Why do I say "may begin"? Science is beginning already to utilise them, for doctors of the Continent of Europe, especially in Paris, are utilising what we call etheric sight in order to diagnose obscure diseases. They mesmerise the person, and get that person to use the finer sight—for you have all got it—to diagnose the disease, which the physical eye cannot see through the muscle and bones of the physical body; they utilise the X rays, without the danger of the ordinary use of X rays. They do not call it clairvoyance. That would not consort with the dignity of the medical profession. They call it internal autoscopy. It does not matter what you call it, only "Clairvoyance" is easier to say. They are beginning to use the finer forces. More and more these forces will be utilised. Why should not the chemist use the finer forces to investigate, when his microscope and balance fail? Some of you know that a very large number of important investigations have been made during the last summer. Nearly sixty chemical elements have been examined by clairvoyance, their forms have been pictured, and diagrams have been made, showing the relation of one part to the other. Chemists are interested in what has been done, and at the present time some are studying these things, in order to see how far chemistry can utilise these investigations, carried much further than chemists have been able to carry their researches hitherto. I am not asking that these observations of ours should be taken as facts, only as reasonable hypotheses; that chemists, when they find a mass of information such as Mr. Leadbeater and myself have been giving them during these late months, entirely made up of clairvoyant observations, should, if they appear to them to be reasonable, use them by experimenting on them. If they can succeed by making discoveries through experiments on these theories, then it will be a fair argument for clairvoyance for us to say: "These things were studied in 1907 by

Theosophical Clairvoyants, and now science is proving them." These are possibilities of helpfulness to orthodox scientists. So with electrical researches. Quite lately I have received—since I have arrived in Australia—a request from one of your own electricians to look clairvoyantly at the X rays and other rays. Scientific men are beginning to wake up to the possibility of things which a few years ago they denied, and it is the duty of those members of the Society who have developed, to some extent at least, these finer organs to put them at the service of scientific men, to observe accurately and record exactly what they see. Although I have studied chemistry, I do not pretend to be a great chemist. I realise that what is valuable in these investigations is not the theories which I might make, but the particular facts which I am able to observe. I leave scientists to make the theories, because they know so much more than I know. These are merely actual observations of, to us, visible things. If chemists find they can be utilised to carry chemical science further than it has been carried yet, so much the better. It will introduce them to the higher possibilities of evolution, and make them less sceptical as to the present evolution of man. You may say to me, and I shall answer straightforwardly: "Is it true that everyone has these powers?" Yes. The proof of it is this: there are a few people you find with these powers when wide awake, but you find, if you mesmerise a person, that almost every person can be made clairvoyant. When you stop the coarser vibrations, the finer are able to assert themselves. That is an absolute fact. But just as you would not hear the delicate notes of a violin in the crash of a motor omnibus, so you cannot hear or feel the finer vibrations of matter when the coarser ones are about you, and you are answering to them. The dulling of the coarser parts of the brain enables the finer parts of the brain to be utilised by yourself, the perceiver. If you find that almost everyone mesmerised is able to see, is it not a fair presumption that that is a common power developing in evolution at the present time? Some people have developed it a little bit ahead of others, but all of us will develop it in time. It is only a question of effort applied along a particular line. People, while practically developing it now, require for high success a certain capacity to begin with, just as you cannot make a senior wrangler out of a boy who cannot understand the simple elements of mathematics. And so with any one of you; unless the mental organs are in a state of high development, you must give the senses time to evolve. Though you may not be able to attain it at once, what I want to leave with you is the idea that it is a natural thing. Presently everybody will have it. Whether any one of you can develop it or not depends on your having a little capacity, on having time and patience, by which you will evolve it more rapidly than nature will do it for you. If you will look at things in that way, that you have not reached the highest point of human evolution, that you have to go higher and higher up this mighty ladder, that you have grown out of the mud far below, that you will climb up to the highest point of the Divine Mountain in the days to come, then it will not seem strange that in the past there have been men above their fellows who have spoken of the realities of the other worlds. Then you will realise the possibility of the prophet and the sage. The more highly these powers are developed in you, the more you will grow up to a higher sense of the dignity of human nature; your future destiny will become more real, your inner powers will become to you more possible of realisation; and so the laws of scientific thought along which I have been trying to lead you will bring you into regions of beauty, of grandeur, of splendour, that at the present time you can scarcely dream of, and you will know the mighty possibilities which lie in the nature of man, a citizen of heaven, although living for a time on earth.